292

D0456903

For current pricing information,
or to learn more about this or any Nextext title,
call us toll-free at **1-800-323-5435**
or visit our web site at www.nextext.com.

STORIES IN HISTORY

ANCIENT GREECE

2000–300 B.C.

Cover illustration: Todd Leonardo

Printed in the United States of America

ISBN 0-618-14211-8

2 3 4 5 6 7 — QKT — 06 05 04 03 02

Table of Contents

PART I: THE FIRST GREEKS

2000–1450 B.C.

by Walter Hazen

*When Leander and his friend travel from Athens
to the island of Crete, they are surprised by
the beautiful palace at Knossos. Although they
don't meet King Minos, they do get to see the
dangerous sport of bull-leaping.*

PART II: DAILY LIFE IN ANCIENT GREECE

PART IV: ART, ARCHITECTURE, AND LITERATURE

Aesop was an ancient Greek storyteller who was famous for his wonderful fables. The responses of an audience of modern children to several of his best-known stories will help you see why.

Some people say that Phidias was one of the greatest sculptors of all time. He was chosen by Pericles to oversee the building of the Parthenon in Athens. He ran into some trouble when the great project was finished, however.

Surely two people can't fight over Greek pottery. Or can they? When Thalassos and Timonium disagree about who is the finest Greek potter, Euphronius or Euthymides, their friendship is shattered.

About this Book

The stories are historical fiction. They are based on historical fact, but some of the characters and events may be fictional. In the Sources section you'll learn which is which and where the information came from.

The illustrations are all historical. If they are from a time different from the story, the caption tells you. Original documents help you understand the time period. Maps let you know where things were.

Items explained in People and Terms to Know are repeated in the Glossary. Look there if you come across a name or term you don't know.

Historians do not always agree on the exact dates of events in the ancient past. The letter c before a date means "about" (from the Latin word circa).

If you would like to read more about these exciting times, you will find recommendations in Reading on Your Own.

Background

We are lovers of the beautiful, yet simple in our tastes, and we cultivate the mind without loss of manliness.

—Pericles on the Athenians

▲
This bronze sculpture pictures the Greek god Poseidon, who ruled the sea.

The First Greeks

> *One of the great islands of the world*
> *in midsea, in the winedark sea, is Crete:*
> *spacious and rich and populous, with ninety*
> *cities and a mingling of tongues.*
>
> —Homer, *The Odyssey*

The history and culture of the Greeks were shaped by the geography of their world. The mainland of Greece is divided by steep mountains and deep valleys. The Greeks also settled hundreds of islands in the surrounding Aegean (ih•JEE•uhn) and Ionian (eye•OH•nee•uhn) seas. Because much of Greece is mountainous, farming has always been hard. So the ancient Greeks turned to the sea for their livelihoods, becoming fishermen, merchants, and sometimes raiders. They sailed to trade or conquer, and spread their civilization throughout the Mediterranean world.

Two Early Civilizations

Two early civilizations had a great influence on the later development of Greece.

Ancient Greece, 2500–300 B.C.

MACEDONIA
Mt. Olympus
•Troy
Thermopylae
(480 B.C.)
Aegean
Sea
Plataea
Delphi (476 B.C.)
ITHAKA
Marathon
Salamis (490 B.C.)
Olympia (480 B.C.) Athens
Ionian •Mycenae
Sea PELOPONNESE
•Sparta
IONIA
KOS
Mediterranean
Sea

0   50   100 Miles

0   100 Kilometers

Knossos
CRETE

N
W—E
S

The Minoans. The first of these was the Minoan
(mih•NOH•uhn) civilization. The Minoans lived
on Crete (kreet), a large island on the southern edge
of the Aegean Sea. Around 2500 B.C., they began to
develop a remarkable civilization. Historians
believe it was a peaceful civilization, since Minoan
cities did not have walls to protect them. In modern
times, archaeologists dug up Knossos (NAHS•uhs),
the Minoan capital city. They found palaces with
richly decorated rooms, beautiful pottery, and other
remains of Minoan civilization.

◀ This golden mask covered the face of a dead Mycenaean king who ruled around 1600 B.C.

The Mycenaeans. Around 2000 B.C. another civilization arose at Mycenae (my•SEE•nee) in the Peloponnese (PEHL•uh•puh•NEES), the southern part of the Greek mainland. Unlike Minoan Crete, the Mycenaean world was not peaceful. Mycenae was located on a steep, rocky ridge and protected by huge walls. The Mycenaeans invaded Crete and helped end Minoan civilization. According to Greek tradition, the Mycenaeans also captured the city of Troy around 1250 B.C. Some 500 years later, the Greek poet Homer described the events of the Trojan War in his epic poems, *The Iliad* and *The Odyssey.*

The Mycenaeans themselves were overrun by invaders from the north. These invasions forced some Greeks to move eastward across the Aegean Sea. There they founded the Greek cities of Ionia.

◀ In this ancient Greek sculpture, the goddess Athena mourns for those killed in battle.

The Rise of the City-States

The geography of Greece, with its mountains and islands, kept the Greeks from forming a single, large country. Instead, they developed small, independent political units called city-states. An ancient Greek city-state was made up of a city and its surrounding countryside, which included numerous villages. These Greek cities were small, often home to fewer than 20,000 people. Some were ruled by kings. Others were controlled by a small group of wealthy, land-owning families. One city-state, Athens, eventually developed a democracy. However, Athenian democracy was very limited. Only free adult males participated in political decision-making. Women, slaves, and foreigners were not citizens and had few rights.

The Persian Wars

Around 500 B.C., Greece was threatened by the growing Persian Empire. (See the map on page 135.) The Persians had conquered the Greek city-states of Ionia. When the Ionians revolted, the Persians crushed them. The Persians then invaded the Greek mainland twice, in 490 and 480 B.C. But the Greeks were able to stop both invasions. Below are the most important battles of the Persian Wars. The Greeks celebrated these wars in their art and literature.

Date	Place	Outcome
490 B.C.	Marathon (MAR•uh•THAHN)	Athenians defeat Persians; runner brings news of victory to Athens in the first "marathon" race.
480 B.C.	Thermopylae (thuhr•MAHP•uh•lee)	Persians destroy small Spartan force, but Spartan sacrifice inspires Greece.
480 B.C.	Salamis (SAL•uh•mihs)	Greek fleet defeats Persians.
479 B.C.	Plataea (pluh•TEE•uh)	Spartans defeat Persians.

Athens and Sparta

The two most important Greek city-states were Athens and Sparta. They were very different societies.

Sparta

Sparta's power was based on its army. The Spartans had an unchanging way of life centered on training for war. At the age of seven, boys left home and moved into army barracks. Wearing no shoes, they marched in light clothing during the day and slept on hard benches at night. Even as adults, male Spartans ate at a mess hall. Although Spartan girls did not receive military training, they ran, wrestled, and played sports to make them tough.

Athens

Athens was very different. Athenian military power was based on its navy. Athenian democracy, though limited, allowed Athens to be a much more open society than Sparta. The Athenians prided themselves on their ability to do many things well. Athenian architects and sculptors created works that stressed order, balance, and proportion. These values became the standards of what is called classical art. Athens also invented drama for Western civilization.

Athenian playwrights used myths and legends to create plays dealing with social issues. Going to the theater was a civic duty. Drama helped the Athenians understand current problems in their society.

War Between Athens and Sparta

The victories of Athens in the Persian Wars made it clear that Athens was the strongest city-state in Greece. In 477 B.C., Athens organized most of the Aegean islands and many Greek cities into the Delian (DEE•lee•uhn) League. They united to protect themselves against further Persian invasions. Athens collected taxes from the members of the League and became wealthy. The city-state was becoming a naval empire.

Sparta was jealous of Athenian power. Sparta declared war on Athens in 431 B.C. With one period of peace, the Peloponnesian War between the two city-states lasted more than twenty years, until 404 B.C. The Spartans eventually won, but their victory was hollow, since it left the Greeks weak. The Greek historian Thucydides (thoo•SIHD•ih•DEEZ) wrote his *History of the Peloponnesian War* to show how Athens and Sparta destroyed themselves because they could not live together in peace.

Philip of Macedonia and Alexander the Great

Greece had been seriously weakened by the Peloponnesian War. Philip of Macedonia was the king of a country to the north of Greece (see the map on page 12). Philip took advantage of this weakness to conquer the Greeks. He was about to invade Persia when he was murdered in 336 B.C. His son, Alexander the Great, carried out Philip's plan. Alexander invaded and conquered the Persian Empire. He then marched eastward

▲
A coin of Alexander the Great.

to India until his war-weary soldiers forced him to turn back. Alexander had big plans to organize and unify the great empire he had conquered. Although he died before he could achieve his goals, his conquests spread Greek civilization over a wide area.

The Heritage of Greece

Someone, I tell you,
Will remember us.

—Sappho

The Greeks created an extraordinary cultural heritage for Western civilization. Greek mythology provided a rich storehouse of subjects for writers and artists. Greek poets such as Sappho introduced the personal voice into literature. Democracy began in Athens. So did European drama. Greeks such as Socrates, Plato, and Aristotle began the type of thinking we call philosophy. Science also began with the Greeks. Greek achievements in sculpture and architecture have shaped Western ideals of beauty. The Greek historian Thucydides, who based his account of the Peloponnesian War on factual evidence and not legend, was the first person to write real history in the modern sense. Above all, the Greeks introduced into Western civilization the idea that the individual person is important.

The Olympian Gods

One thing that united the Greeks was their mythology. The chief Greek gods were believed to live on Mount Olympus, a high mountain in northern Greece. These are their names, relationships, and functions:

Zeus (zoos)—god of the sky; king of the gods and human beings.

Hera (HEER•uh)—sister and wife of Zeus; queen of the gods.

Hestia (HEHS•tee•uh)—sister of Zeus; goddess of the fireside.

Poseidon (poh•SYD•n)—brother of Zeus; god of the sea.

Hades (HAY•deez)—brother of Zeus; ruler of the world of the dead.

Demeter (dih•MEE•tuhr)—sister of Zeus; goddess of the harvest.

Athena (uh•THEE•nuh)—daughter of Zeus; goddess of wisdom and war.

Ares (AIR•eez)—son of Zeus and Hera; god of war.

Hephaestus (hih•FEHS•tuhs)—son of Zeus and Hera; god of fire.

Aphrodite (AF•ruh•DY•tee)—daughter of Zeus; goddess of love and beauty.

Hermes (HUR•meez)—son of Zeus; messenger of the gods.

Apollo (uh•PAHL•oh)—son of Zeus; god of the sun, poetry, music, archery, and healing.

Artemis (AHR•tuh•mihs)—daughter of Zeus and sister of Apollo; goddess of the moon, the hunt, forests, and wild animals.

Dionysus (DY•uh•NY•suhs)—son of Zeus; god of wine.

Time Line

c. 2500–1400 b.c.—Minoan civilization is at
    its height.

c. 1600–1200 b.c.—Mycenaean civilization
    is at its height.

c. 1450 b.c.—Mycenaeans invade Crete.

c. 1250 b.c.—The Trojan War is fought.

776 b.c.—The first Olympic games are held.

c. 750–700 b.c.—Homer composes *The Iliad*
    and *The Odyssey*.

c. 500–479 b.c.—The Persians wage war
    against the Greeks.

490 b.c.—The Greeks defeat the Persians
    at Marathon.

480 b.c.—The Spartans make an heroic defense
    against the Persians at Thermopylae.

477 b.c.—Athens establishes the Delian League.

461–429 b.c.—Pericles dominates Athens.

c. 460 B.C.—Hippocrates is born.

447–432 B.C.—The Parthenon is built.

438 B.C.—Phidias's statue of Athena is dedicated.

431–404 B.C.—The Peloponnesian War is fought.

430–411 B.C.—Thucydides writes his *History of the Peloponnesian War.*

399 B.C.—Socrates is tried and put to death.

338 B.C.—Philip of Macedonia conquers Greece.

336 B.C.—Alexander becomes king of Macedonia.

331 B.C.—Alexander the Great conquers Persia.

323 B.C.—Alexander dies in Babylon.

▲
The Parthenon in Athens is the temple of the city's patron goddess, Athena.
This building expresses the qualities of grace and balance that are central to
the Greek ideal of beauty.

The First Greeks

The Palace at Knossos

BY WALTER HAZEN

The Minoan civilization on the island of **Crete** was named for him. Was there really a King **Minos**? Did he live in a magnificent palace outside the city of Knossos?

The answers to the above questions are "probably not" and "yes." The ruler of the island of Crete did live in a great palace. Its description makes up the better part of this story. As to King Minos being real, some historians think there may have been

---

People and Terms to Know

Crete (kreet)—island of southeast Greece in the eastern Mediterranean Sea. Its Minoan (mih•NOH•uhn) civilization was one of the earliest in the world. It reached the height of wealth and power around 1600 B.C.

Minos (MY•nuhs)—legendary king of Crete. He was said to be the son of Zeus, the supreme god of the Greeks, and Europa, a Phoenician princess. The ancient Greeks believed he had ruled several generations before the Trojan War, that is, around 1325 B.C.

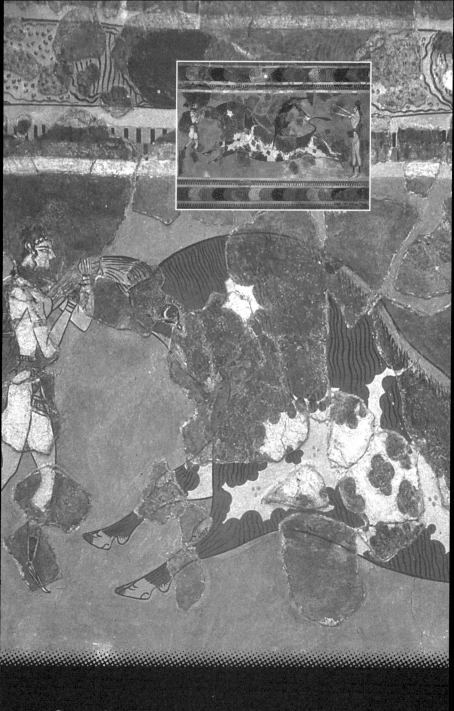

One young Minoan grasps a bull's horns to prepare for a leap. The inset
shows how a second somersaults over the back of the animal and a third
waits to help the vaulter land.

several kings by that name. Others believe "Minos" was nothing more than a title given to the kings of Crete.

Perhaps King Minos was only legendary, but people centuries ago thought he was very real.

* * *

I could not believe my good fortune. Here I stood at the entrance to the beautiful palace at **Knossos**. Would I see the great king? Would I be allowed to explore the many halls and rooms of the palace?

"Look!" I pointed out to my friend, Leander. "Look at those bright colors. Have you ever seen such blues, such reds, such yellows!"

"They are striking," replied Leander. "And look at the columns. They look as though they're upside down. See how they are broad at the top and taper down toward the bottom."

"They are unusual," I agreed.

People and Terms to Know

Knossos (NAHS•uhs)—ancient city of northern Crete.

Leander and I stood in awe at the sight before us. Nothing in **Athens** could compare with this magnificent palace. We Athenians, in fact, seem backward compared to the civilization that has arisen on Crete. Perhaps its greatness is due to its location. Being an island nation, it has had little to worry about from invaders. Its people have been left alone to devote their energy to the arts and other peaceful activities.

Nothing in Athens could compare with this magnificent palace.

Leander and I had come to Knossos on a trade mission. As things turned out, we did not get to see King Minos. But we really did not expect to. We met with one of his advisers. After our business was over, the adviser took us on a tour of the palace.

As we began our tour, our guide told us something of the palace's size. He said the three-story building covered six acres. It measured 150 square meters (492 square feet) and was built around an open courtyard. The courtyard was rectangular in

People and Terms to Know

Athens (ATH•uhnz)—city in the ancient region of Attica on the mainland of Greece, now the capital and largest city of Greece. People who live in Athens are called *Athenians* (uh•THEE•nee•uhnz).

shape and was about 50 meters (164 feet) long. The whole structure was made of sun-dried brick and wood.

We quickly discovered that the palace contained many passageways that led to offices, storerooms, apartments, corridors, staircases, and rows of columns.

"Boy!" cried Leander. "One could easily get lost in this place."

As I walked, I wondered if these passageways made up the Labyrinth.

I agreed. As I walked, I wondered if these passageways made up the **Labyrinth** where **Theseus** was supposed to have killed the Minotaur. Certainly, Minos could have kept the monster here, and it would have never found its way out. I was about to ask our guide about this when he hurried off on some business and left us to ourselves.

Many things about the palace left us spellbound. We could not believe that its rooms came complete with running water and toilets that

People and Terms to Know

Labyrinth (LAB•uh•rihnth)—in Greek mythology, the maze or group of complicated passageways where the hero Theseus killed the Minotaur (MIHN•uh•tawr), a monster that had the head of a bull and the body of a man.

Theseus (THEE•see•uhs)—in Greek mythology, a hero and king of Athens.

The Minoans created vivid images of the natural world in their art, like the octopus on this vase. ▶

flushed! And the **<u>frescoes</u>**! Never had we seen such beautiful wall paintings. The pictures show the Minoans as they are: a happy, peaceful people who enjoy life to the fullest. In one long passageway called the Corridor of the Procession, there is a colorful fresco showing a parade. There are priests and priestesses. There are handsome young men and beautiful young girls. There are wealthy landowners and farmers. Every walk of life is represented in this series of paintings.

Other paintings show events with women alongside men. Unlike Athens, where our women must stay at home, Minoan women go where they please. They seem to enjoy the same rights as Minoan men.

People and Terms to Know

frescoes (FREHS•kohs)—paintings done on fresh moist plaster with colors dissolved in water.

Some of the younger women take part in bull-leaping. In this sport, a boy or girl grabs the horns of a charging bull and does a somersault or handspring over its back. A companion often runs along behind the bull to steady the leaper as he or she jumps to the ground.

Were they slaves or captives forced to perform?

While Leander and I were at the palace, we were treated to a special performance of bull-leaping. It was staged in the open court of the palace. I must admit I felt fearful the first time I saw a young girl grasp a bull's horns and go into her somersault.

"Are any of these performers ever hurt?" I nervously asked a man standing next to me on a balcony overlooking the court.

"Oh, yes," he replied. "Occasionally someone is badly hurt or even killed. But that doesn't happen often. These boys and girls are good athletes."

I was curious about the background of these young people. Were they slaves or captives forced to perform? When I asked the man about this, he told me that the boys and girls come from some of Crete's best families. Some of the girls are even princesses.

Although bull-leaping is a sport, it proves how important bulls are in Minoan custom and religion. Leander and I had noticed them not only on wall paintings but on vases and other art objects as well. This is probably because Zeus changed himself into a white bull when he dashed off to Crete with **Europa**.

Leander and I left Crete with nothing but admiration for the Minoans. Here are a people far more advanced than us Greeks. I'm sure we will learn much from them.

QUESTIONS TO CONSIDER

1. How would you explain what a myth is?

2. Why do you think people are not sure whether there really was a King Minos?

3. Why were the narrator and Leander impressed by the palace at Knossos?

4. What is your opinion of the sport of bull-leaping?

People and Terms to Know

Europa (yoo•ROH•puh)—legendary Phoenician princess. She was kidnapped by the god Zeus (who had changed himself into a white bull) and taken to Crete. Minos was their son. The continent of Europe is named for her.

A Story of Buried Treasure

BY BARBARA LITTMAN

During early 1870, **Heinrich Schliemann** explored the hot, dusty plains on the eastern shore of the **Aegean Sea**. He carried with him a dog-eared copy of *The Iliad* by **Homer**. He compared everything he saw to Homer's description of **Troy**.

People and Terms to Know

Heinrich Schliemann (HYN•rihk SHLEE•mahn)—(1822–1890) German amateur archaeologist who discovered the lost city of Troy by using Homer's *Iliad* to identify the site.

Aegean (ih•JEE•uhn) **Sea**—arm of the Mediterranean Sea between Greece and Turkey. It is dotted with islands. See the map on page 12.

Homer (HOH•muhr)—Greek poet and author of two long poems, *The Iliad* and *The Odyssey*, composed around 750 B.C. *The Iliad* tells of Troy and the Trojan War. *The Odyssey* tells of the adventures of Odysseus, king of Ithaca.

Troy—ancient city of northwest Asia Minor and the legendary place of the Trojan War. The people of Troy were called *Trojans*. The Trojan War between the Greeks and the Trojans lasted ten years. The ruins of Troy were first discovered by Heinrich Schliemann.

The jewelry and other objects that Heinrich Schliemann found at Hisarlik were exhibited in a London museum in 1877.

When he saw **Hisarlik** hill, he thought it matched Homer's description. Troy had been on high land, just like Hisarlik. Homer wrote of the number of trips the Greek soldiers could make in a day from their boat to the city. Hisarlik's distance from the sea was about like Troy's. A mountain range was also described in just the right place, with one peak higher than the others.

For ten long years the Greek fighting men had battled to take over Troy.

When Heinrich Schliemann was a boy, his father had given him a history book. Heinrich had loved the stories of the brave Greek warriors. He had especially liked Homer's story. In this story, the Greeks had sailed to Troy to take back Helen, their king's beautiful wife. She had run off with Paris, the son of King **Priam**, the king of Troy. For ten long years the Greek fighting men had battled to take over Troy. It was a wonderful tale of romance and heroism that no child could resist.

But no one seemed to know whether Troy had ever really existed. Curious and intelligent, Heinrich

---

People and Terms to Know

Hisarlik (hih•sahr•LIHK)—modern site of ancient Troy in the present-day country of Turkey.

Priam (PRY•uhm)—in Greek mythology, the king of Troy, who was killed when his city fell to the Greeks.

decided that when he grew up he would find the lost city of Troy.

In 1871, convinced that he had found the location of the lost city of Troy, Heinrich Schliemann started to dig. He hired workers to help him and had a deep trench dug into the side of the hill. Almost immediately, he uncovered stone walls that were six feet thick and skillfully built. Much to his surprise, the trench revealed walls on top of walls. He realized that he had uncovered cities built on top of cities. Convinced that Homer's Troy must be the oldest city, he quickly dug down to the bottom.

Unfortunately, Schliemann was wrong. The Troy Homer described was not at the bottom. It was much closer to the top, so large portions of Homer's Troy were destroyed when the trench was dug. Schliemann did not realize what he had done, though, and he continued his digging. At many times, his wife Sophia worked with him. In May 1873, he uncovered what he thought were the walls of King Priam's palace. There were paved streets, huge clay storage jars, and what looked like parts of large gates.

He was to find something even more amazing, however. In the process of digging, he later wrote, he saw a "large copper article of the most remarkable form, which attracted my attention all the more as I thought I saw gold behind it. . . ."

He carefully dug around the object, which proved to be a large shield. He also found a gold bottle, several gold cups, copper daggers, vases, gold necklaces and headpieces, and many small pieces of gold jewelry. Schliemann was convinced he had discovered the treasure of King Priam.

Schliemann was convinced he had discovered the treasure of King Priam.

Today, we know that the Troy where Schliemann found his gold treasures was not the Troy Homer had written about. Schliemann had dug down so far, he was about a thousand years too early. Homer's Troy was probably the sixth city in the layers of cities. The evidence shows that it was destroyed by a large fire. Some scholars say this fact supports the idea that the Trojan War really happened.

Heinrich Schliemann was an intelligent, imaginative man who made many contributions to the field of **archaeology**. Some people say that some of the things he said and wrote were not true,

People and Terms to Know

archaeology (AHR•kee•AHL•uh•jee)—finding and study of the remains of past human life. These remains might be graves, buildings, tools, jewelry, or pottery. The person who finds and studies these remains is called an *archaeologist* (AHR•kee•AHL•uh•jihst).

▲

These daggers inlaid with gold were found in graves that Schliemann discovered in ancient Mycenae. See page 13.

however. Other people criticize his methods of archaeology because he mixed up his findings from the different layers of cities.

No matter what people think of his honesty or skill, Schliemann was the first person to use an ancient story to locate archaeological evidence. Without his work, it is possible we still wouldn't know whether the city of Troy had ever really existed. As important, without the treasures he unearthed there, we would not understand what daily life was like in that part of the world thousands of years ago.

QUESTIONS TO CONSIDER

1. How did Heinrich Schliemann find Troy?

2. Why did some people find fault with Schliemann?

3. What did you learn about Troy from reading this story?

4. What do you think are some things one has to know to become an archaeologist?

The Greeks and Troy
by Deborah Tyler

Deborah Tyler introduces the ancient city of Troy through discoveries made by Heinrich Schliemann and other archaeologists.

In Search of Troy: One Man's Quest for Homer's Fabled City
by Giovanni Caselli

Giovanni Caselli presents the story of Heinrich Schliemann, the German amateur archaeologist whose boyhood fascination with Homer's epics sent him on a search to discover the actual remains of ancient Troy.

The Mysteries of Troy
by I. G. Edmonds

I. G. Edmonds shares the history, literature and legends, archaeology, and art of ancient Troy.

The Trojan War

BY JUDY VOLEM

The soldiers of Troy gathered on the towers of their city and looked down upon the strange creature that stood at the gate. An enormous wooden horse appeared ready to enter. But for what purpose?

Helen _stood_ _alone,_ _gazing_ _at_ _the_ _remains_ _of_ _the_ _deserted Greek camp. The sleek wooden ships that had_ _been beached on the shore nearby were gone. Smoke rose_ _from the huts the Greeks had burned when they left._ _Dogs sniffed around the ashes. Helen wondered if this_ _truly meant the end of the war that had dragged on for_ _ten years._

People and Terms to Know

Helen—In Homer's _Iliad_, she is the wife of the king of Sparta. The Trojan War is said to have started because of her.

This is how an artist of the 1800s pictured Paris, the Trojan prince, carrying off Helen, the Greek queen of Sparta.

As she looked upon the plain and the sea beyond, Helen's thoughts drifted into the past. At which moment had all the troubles begun? She felt great sorrow and responsibility for the long suffering.

It started at a wedding many years ago with a quarrel among the gods. The goddess of discord had not been invited. To make trouble, she threw a golden apple among the guests. Written on it were the words "For the fairest." She knew that would stir up competition among the three most glorious goddesses, **Athena**, **Hera**, and **Aphrodite**. Indeed, each saw herself as the obvious owner of the apple. That was the seed of all the troubles to follow.

Not even **Zeus**, the ruler of the gods, wanted to choose the fairest for fear of angering the other two. So he set the task of judgment to handsome young **Paris** of Troy.

People and Terms to Know

Athena (uh•THEE•nuh)—goddess of wisdom and warfare.

Hera (HEER•uh)—wife of Zeus, ruler of the gods.

Aphrodite (AF•ruh•DY•tee)—goddess of love and beauty.

Zeus (zoos)—in Greek mythology, god of the sky and king of the gods and human beings.

Paris (PAIR•ihs)—son of the king of Troy. When he ran off with Helen, the Trojan War started.

Each goddess tried to bribe the young prince to get the golden apple. Athena pledged that he would be the wisest of men. Hera promised Paris that he would be the most powerful ruler of all. Aphrodite offered him the love of the most beautiful woman in the world.

Paris, young and foolish, chose Aphrodite's gift. All agreed that Helen was the most beautiful woman on earth. It wasn't important to Aphrodite that Helen was already married to

Each goddess tried to bribe the young prince to get the golden apple.

Menelaus, king of Sparta. Aphrodite cast a spell that caused Helen to fall in love with Paris and run away with him to Troy.

Helen remembered the seasick feeling of her love for Paris. She couldn't deny him. She wondered now how she could have left her child and broken her marriage promise to Menelaus.

When Menelaus realized Helen's betrayal, he gathered together the great warriors of Greece. With 1,000 black ships, Menelaus set off to get back his wife and destroy the city of Troy. He believed he would be

People and Terms to Know

Menelaus (MEHN•uh•LAY•uhs)—in Greek mythology, the king of Sparta at the time of the Trojan War and husband of Helen.

victorious. His brother **Agamemnon** could gather and lead the Greek army. Not only did Menelaus have the support of such great warriors as **Odysseus** and **Achilles**, he had the help of Hera and Athena as well. The goddesses would take their revenge on Paris.

The Greek soldiers prepared to conquer the city that held the beautiful Helen.

Many rowers pulled the ships through stormy seas. They landed on the beaches and saw the city of Troy towering above the plain. The Greek soldiers prepared to conquer the city that held the beautiful Helen. Lines of men in polished armor and holding heavy spears and shields ran forward to attack. They couldn't break through the thick walls and well-guarded gates. The soldiers retreated from the showers of arrows.

When the Greeks realized they would not easily destroy Troy, they settled down for a long **siege**. They listened to clever Odysseus and raided neighboring

---

People and Terms to Know

Agamemnon (AG•uh•MEHM•nahn)—in Greek mythology, king of the Greek city of Mycenae (my•SEE•nee).

Odysseus (oh•DIHS•yoos)—in Greek mythology, the king of Ithaca. The story of his adventures after the Trojan War is told in Homer's *Odyssey*.

Achilles (uh•KIHL•eez)—hero of Homer's *Iliad* and the killer of Hector, the greatest Trojan warrior.

siege (seej)—surrounding of a city by an army trying to capture it.

towns. For nine long years they invaded villages along the coast. They gathered supplies for themselves and weakened Troy's allies.

For nine long years, they camped outside Troy. In the tenth year the Greeks again prepared to face the Trojans. However, the greatest Greek fighter, mighty Achilles, refused to take part. After an argument with Agamemnon, Achilles had retreated to his ships. His absence gave the Trojans hope of victory, and they welcomed a battle with the Greeks.

It could have ended there, thought Helen, if Aphrodite had not interfered. **Hector** *convinced his brother Paris to face Menelaus alone on the field of battle. Their duel would have decided my fate.*

But when it looked as if Paris would be struck down by Menelaus's sword, Aphrodite made him invisible. She spirited Paris away back to Troy.

Helen remembered the disgust she had felt for his cowardice. She might have left Paris then, if Aphrodite hadn't again cast her love spell.

The war did not end then. Fierce fighting continued. Men died while the gods took sides and helped their favorites. The Trojans swarmed toward

People and Terms to Know

Hector—son of Priam, king of Troy; the greatest of the Trojan warriors.

the Greek ships, fighting spear to spear. Fire started among the Greek ships. A Trojan victory seemed likely.

Through all of this, Achilles remained apart and refused to join the battle. Then his best friend, Patroclus (puh•TROH•kluhs), put on Achilles's armor and went into battle. Patroclus hoped the Trojans would think that Achilles had returned. But Hector killed Patroclus with a quick thrust of his spear. Now Achilles was ready to carry the rage of a thousand men in his own spear.

Hector stopped and faced Achilles's fearful spear.

Achilles rode into battle, destroying everything in his way. He leaped from his chariot when he saw Hector on the bloody battlefield. Brave Hector stood fast until Achilles rushed at him. Suddenly, Hector's courage vanished. He turned and ran. He ran swiftly around the walls of Troy with Achilles close upon him.

As suddenly as he'd started to run, Hector stopped and faced Achilles's fearful spear. He died with honor.

In anger, Achilles dragged Hector's naked body behind his chariot through the dust and blood of the battlefield and then left him unburied. This was the worst possible insult to a hero. Priam himself, king of Troy and Hector's father, went to Achilles. On bended knee he begged for the return of his son's body. Achilles's heart was touched. He agreed, and

French painting done in the 1800s shows Greek soldiers climbing out of the Trojan Horse to open the gates of Troy to the other Greeks waiting outside.

Priam returned to Troy with Hector's body and gave his son a proper burial.

The war continued with many losses on both sides. An arrow shot by Paris struck Achilles in the heel, the only place on his body where he could be wounded. Paris, too, met his death from a swift and poisonous arrow.

Now, Helen hoped, the war must be over. The Greeks hadn't broken through the walls of Troy. They had sailed off in the night, leaving the great wooden horse as an offering to the goddess Athena.

But what was all the noise? Helen wondered. Princess **<u>Cassandra</u>** *was shouting to make herself heard over the*

People and Terms to Know

Cassandra (kuh•SAN•druh)—in Greek mythology, a daughter of King Priam of Troy. She could foresee the future, but no one ever believed her predictions.

rejoicing of the Trojans. "The wooden horse is a trick of the Greeks!" It was said that Cassandra could see the future, but no one listened to her.

The Trojans should have paid attention to Cassandra's words, for she was right. The Trojans brought the horse in through the gates and up to the temple of Athena. Hidden inside the belly of the giant horse were the bravest of the Greek soldiers. In the middle of the night, they climbed down quietly and opened the gates for their comrades. The Greeks killed all within their reach and finally, in the tenth year, destroyed the city of Troy.

Fair Helen was spared the fate of other women who were carried off as slaves. Odysseus bargained for her life, and she sailed away with Menelaus. As she stood on the deck of the ship, she watched the dark smoke rise from the ruins of Troy.

QUESTIONS TO CONSIDER

1. What was the cause of the Trojan War according to the story?

2. What part did Aphrodite play in the war?

3. Why do you think the people of Troy were tricked by the Trojan Horse?

4. Why do you think the story of the Trojan War continues to interest people?

Greek Tradition

Homer and History Homer composed his epic poems about the Trojan War around 750 B.C. The Greeks of his time believed that their ancestors had fought a ten-year war against the Trojans about 500 years earlier, that is, around 1250 B.C. For many years, historians thought that the legendary stories of the Trojan War were totally fictional. Beginning around 1870 with the work of Heinrich Schliemann, archaeological discoveries suggested that the stories of the Trojan War may have been based on real cities, people, and events.

▲

This carving from an ancient Greek storage jar is the earliest surviving image of the Trojan Horse. It dates from around the time of Homer.

Dateline: Troy
by Paul Fleischman

Paul Fleischman both retells the ancient tale of the Trojan War and shows its timelessness by matching the legendary episodes with accounts of recent events drawn from newspapers.

Black Ships Before Troy: The Story of the Iliad
by Rosemary Sutcliff

The award-winning author of historical fiction for young people retells the story of the Trojan War.

Inside the Walls of Troy: A Novel of the Women Who Lived the Trojan War
by Clemence McLaren

In this novel, Clemence McLaren presents the story of the Trojan War through the eyes of two women, Helen and Cassandra.

Contests with the Amazons

BY LYNNETTE BRENT

Long, long ago, according to Greek <u>legend</u>, a nation of warrior women lived on the southern shore of the Black Sea. The women were called <u>**Amazons**</u>. Only the daughters of the Amazons lived with them. Sons were killed or sent to live with their fathers.

The Amazons fought against the Greek heroes who lived before the Trojan War. Later, they went to help the Trojans in their long war against the Greeks.

Theseus, the king of Athens, was the first Greek hero to meet the Amazons. Always on the

---

People and Terms to Know

legend (LEHJ·uhnd)—story about great deeds handed down from the past. A legend cannot be proved to be true, but it is often believed by many people.

Amazons—in Greek legend, members of a nation of women warriors.

This ancient vase painting shows Greeks fighting Amazons. The Amazon warrior in the center wears clothing resembling that of the Persians the Greeks had fought. See page 15.

lookout for a good contest, Theseus went to the country of the Amazons and captured **Hippolyta**, their queen. Theseus took her back to Greece and forced her to marry him. They had a son named Hippolytus. Soon, Theseus fell in love with another woman. Determined to rescue their queen, the Amazons invaded Athens. They succeeded in taking Hippolyta back to their country.

Determined to rescue their queen, the Amazons invaded Athens.

The second Greek hero to meet the Amazons was the strong man **Hercules**. The goddess Hera had given him twelve hard labors, or tasks, to perform. One of the tasks was to capture the golden belt of Hippolyta, which had been given to the Amazon by her father, the god of war. Hercules sailed from Greece to the Amazons' land. When he reached the queen, she asked him to wrestle with her to prove his strength.

Hera, Hercules's stepmother, hated him. She disguised herself as an Amazon and spread the word that Hercules was attacking Hippolyta. The

---

People and Terms to Know

Hippolyta (hih•PAHL•ih•tuh)—in Greek mythology, a queen of the Amazons.

Hercules (HUR•kyuh•LEEZ)—in Greek and Roman mythology, a son of Zeus. He won immortality, or endless life, by performing 12 tasks demanded by the goddess Hera. The Greek form of his name is *Heracles*.

other Amazons gathered their weapons and attacked Hercules's ship. When word of the attack reached Hercules, he thought that Hippolyta had played a trick on him. He killed her and ripped the belt from her dead body. The war that this act started between the Amazons and Greek armies was terrible. In the end, the Amazons lost.

*   *   *

The early Greek historian **Herodotus** wrote about the Amazons. He was recording legend, however, rather than what he personally saw. Herodotus told the tale of a group of Amazons who were captured after the war with Greece. When they were put on Greek ships, the Amazons murdered the Greeks. Since the Amazons did not know how to sail, they were blown to an island. Here they found a herd of horses. They mounted them and rode off. Living on the island were some

---

People and Terms to Know

Herodotus (hih•RAHD•uh•tuhs)—(c.484–c.425 B.C.) Greek historian known as "the Father of History." He wrote a history of the war between the Greeks and the Persians.

◄ A woman warrior appears on an ancient Greek vase.

nomadic people called **Scythians**. These Scythian men wanted the Amazons as wives, but the Amazons refused. Herodotus wrote that the Amazons replied this way:

> We and the women of your nation could never live together. We are riders; our business is with the bow and spear, and we know nothing of women's work; but in your country no woman has anything to do with such things. Your women stay at home in their wagons occupied with women's tasks, and never go out to hunt or for any other purpose. We could not possibly agree.

People and Terms to Know

nomadic (noh•MAD•ihk)—related to people who move according to the season in search of food, water, and land for their animals to graze on.
Scythians (SIHTH•ee•uhns)—people who lived in an area that extended from the mouth of the Danube River on the Black Sea and on eastward.

The Scythian men were persuaded to travel away with the Amazons to another country.

* * *

Did warrior women exist? Archaeologists have found tombs in southern Russia. In them women are buried along with armor and war horses. These tombs are in the region of the Black Sea, where the ancient Greeks carried on trade. Perhaps they heard of these warrior princesses. If so, they must have believed they were descended from the Amazons.

For more than 2,000 years, people have been fascinated by the idea of such women. They are a favorite subject of writers, artists, sculptors, and moviemakers. Even today, the word *Amazon* inspires the imagination.

QUESTIONS TO CONSIDER

1. Why do you think the legends of the Amazons were popular with artists and historians?

2. What do you think the name *Amazon* on a product or service is meant to tell you?

3. What is your opinion of women warriors?

Amazons
by John K. Anderson

John K. Anderson uses the art of ancient Greece to show how Greek views of these warrior women changed over time.

Fa Mulan: The Story of a Woman Warrior
by Robert D. San Souci

Other cultures also had traditions of women warriors like the Amazons. Robert D. San Souci retells the famous Chinese legend of the brave girl who disguises herself as a boy and takes her father's place in the emperor's army fighting invaders.

The Random House Book of Greek Myths
by Joan Vinge

Joan Vinge retells the story of the Twelve Labors of Hercules, including his capture of the golden belt of the Amazon queen Hippolyta.

Daily Life in
Ancient Greece

Penelope and
the Suitors

BY STEPHEN FEINSTEIN

One night last week, I was working late, as usual. In my rooms, logs were burning in the fireplace to ward off the chill in the air. Though it is summer here on the island of **Ithaca**, a cool mist often drifts in from the sea at night and settles on the olive groves. The mist even creeps through the gates in the high stone walls of the courtyard.

As I said, I am always hard at work at night, carefully unraveling all that I have woven during the day. In the mornings, I spin my fine white wool into yarn. At noon my servant Eurycleia (yoo•RIH•klee•uh) helps me sort the yarn for weaving. Then in the afternoon, I weave the yarn that I have spun.

People and Terms to Know

Ithaca (IHTH•uh•kuh)—one of the islands in the Ionian Sea off western Greece and the legendary home of Odysseus and Penelope. See the map on page 12.

Penelope works at her loom as the men who want to marry her bring gifts in an English painting done in 1912.

I have been carrying on in this fashion for three years. That was when the **suitors** descended upon our home and demanded that I, **Penelope**, queen of Ithaca, choose one of them as my next husband. My dear husband, Odysseus (oh•DIHS•yoos), has been gone twenty years. But I have never given up hope that someday he will return to me.

I have been weaving the shroud for three years!

Odysseus went off to war against the Trojans. The Greeks won! After ten years of fighting, many brave men had died, but not my Odysseus. The Greeks set sail for home, and many have returned, but not my husband. Nobody knows what happened to him after his ships sailed from Troy.

I have told the suitors that I could not make any decision until I finished weaving a shroud for my father-in-law, Laertes (lay•UR•teez). He will be wrapped in it at his death. So far, I have been weaving the shroud for three years! Meanwhile, the suitors, all one hundred of them, make our lives miserable. Old Laertes has gone off in disgust to live on his farm in the hills.

People and Terms to Know

suitors—men who want to marry Penelope.
Penelope (puh•NEHL•uh•pee)—faithful wife of Odysseus.

The suitors, young men from wealthy families, spend all their days at our home. At night they stagger home drunk, only to show up again the next day in time for lunch. They are noisy and rude, ordering my servants around and demanding nightly feasts. Worst of all, they treat my son, **Telemachus**, with contempt. He has just come of age and will soon inherit his father's lands. Yet every day, he has to witness our uninvited guests eating up his inheritance. One day, Telemachus dared to address the suitors and demanded that they leave. They only laughed in his face. So this is the unhappy way we live.

Every evening after the suitors are gone, I get busy unraveling the shroud. That night, it was getting late. I yawned a few times. I was so caught up in my work that I didn't hear the footsteps on the stairs. Suddenly, the door burst open, and in walked Antinous (AN•tih•nuhs), the loudest and most annoying of the suitors! Two others followed him.

"So this is why the shroud is not finished!" exclaimed Antinous. He did not seem surprised, although he was angry.

"How did you know?" I asked, shaken.

People and Terms to Know

Telemachus (tuh•LEHM•uh•kuhs)—son of Penelope and Odysseus.

"One of your servants told me," said Antinous. "Now you must finish the shroud and make your choice. We will never leave this house until you do so. Odysseus himself, should he return from the dead, cannot save you now." With that, Antinous and the others left. I could hear them laughing as they went down the stairs. From then on, I knew I could only expect the worst from them.

> "Odysseus himself, should he return from the dead, cannot save you now."

Several days later, another of the suitors came to me with very disturbing news. He had overheard Antinous and some of the others plotting to kill my son! It seems they had decided that Telemachus disapproved of them and would urge me never to marry any of them. I went downstairs and through the women's quarters into the great hall beyond. The suitors were gathered there. "It's the queen!" one of them shouted. They grew quiet.

"Antinous, how could you plan such evil?" I cried. "Have you no shame?"

Antinous refused to admit anything. One of the other suitors, Eurymachus (yoo•RIHM•uh•kuhs), defended him. He suggested that somebody was purposely trying to poison me against the suitors.

"Queen Penelope, we all have the highest regard for Telemachus," he said. I left them, convinced that they were lying.

Yesterday I was dining, as usual, in my rooms. I could hear the loud sounds of the nightly party. One of my servants came to me and said, "My lady, there's an old man in the hall, a beggar. He wishes to speak to you. He says he fought at your husband's side at Troy." My heart skipped a beat. Could this beggar truly tell me about my husband? I told the servant to make sure the man was given food and drink.

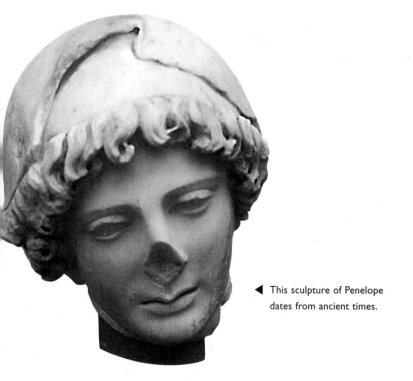

◀ This sculpture of Penelope dates from ancient times.

▲
This ancient Greek sculpture shows the beggar talking to Penelope.

When the suitors had departed, I went downstairs to the hall. I saw that Telemachus and the beggar were having a friendly conversation. When my son saw me, he said goodnight and left. My maids set a chair for the old man beside the fire, close to mine. He was dressed in rags, yet there was something strangely familiar about him. When I asked him to tell me about himself, he refused, saying that he had suffered too much. So I told him all about my troubled times. When I asked him about Odysseus, he had nothing but praise for my husband. Then he described the clothing Odysseus had worn, including the purple cloak fastened with a golden pin in the shape of a hound bringing down a deer. Tears came to my eyes. The old man had indeed known my husband.

"Your husband will return home soon," said the old man. I wanted to believe him. By then, though, I feared I would have to marry one of the suitors. I told the beggar that the next day I would announce a competition. I would marry the man who could string Odysseus's great bow and then shoot an arrow through a row of ax heads. The old man agreed that this was a good plan.

One by one, the suitors each tried and failed to string the bow.

Today the suitors were eager for the competition to begin. A dozen axes had been set up in a line. One by one, the suitors each tried and failed to string the bow. Antinous, the only one who had yet to try his luck, hesitated. "Let's wait until tomorrow," he said, "and then we can all try again."

Just then, the old beggar asked if he could try the bow. Antinous and the other suitors laughed. They told the old man to stop bothering them. This made me angry. "The stranger is our guest, Antinous. It is not for you to say what he can or cannot do," I said.

Before I could continue, Telemachus said, "Mother, since the bow belonged to my father, I should be the one to decide who should touch the bow. Please go to your rooms and your weaving. The handling of bows is the responsibility of men, not women."

I was surprised by my son's words. Now he had spoken like a man! I left the great hall, taking Eurycleia and the maids with me. I went up to my rooms and began weaving. Shortly after that, a great commotion began in the hall. I could hear shouting and screaming. I became alarmed and ran downstairs. I couldn't get into the hall because somebody had locked the doors. Something terrible was happening in there, and my Telemachus was inside. I could hear objects, perhaps bodies, crashing to the floor. Beside myself with worry, I went back upstairs and prayed to the gods. I thought about my absent husband and started to weep. Finally, I fell asleep.

The next thing I knew, I was being shaken awake by Eurycleia. "Odysseus has come home, and all the suitors are dead!" she cried. I rubbed my eyes and stared at her.

"Either I'm still dreaming, or you have gone mad," I said.

"It's true!" Eurycleia said. "Odysseus and your son have slain the suitors!"

As I sat up, Telemachus and the old beggar entered my rooms. His wrinkles were gone, and his white hair was now black! For a long time I just stared at the man. Was this Odysseus? Sometimes I seemed to see my husband. Sometimes the man seemed a stranger. To make sure this man was really my husband, I told Eurycleia to make up his bed and move it outside the bedroom.

"Who has dared to move my bed?" the stranger said angrily.

"Who has dared to move my bed?" the stranger said angrily. "No one can move that bed. One of the bedposts is made from the trunk of an olive tree, still standing in the ground. I made that bed myself."

I knew then that the gods had answered my prayers. Before me stood Odysseus, my dear husband! We threw our arms around each other, tears flowing from our eyes. We would have much to talk about.

QUESTIONS TO CONSIDER

1. Why did Penelope unravel all of the weaving she had done each day?

2. What responsibilities did Penelope have in her home?

3. What qualities do you think made Penelope an ideal woman to the ancient Greeks?

4. Why do you think Antinous decided to wait until the next day to take his turn with the bow?

5. Why didn't Penelope recognize her husband?

6. If you had been in Penelope's situation, would you have waited such a long time to marry again?

The Legend of Odysseus
by Peter Connolly

Peter Connolly both retells Homer's Iliad *and* Odyssey *and describes the civilization of the Greek world at the time of Odysseus.*

Aleta and the Queen
by Priscilla Galloway

In this historical novel, Priscilla Galloway retells part of Homer's Odyssey. *She describes the final weeks before the hero's return through the eyes of Aleta, the 12-year-old granddaughter of Penelope's housekeeper.*

Waiting for Odysseus: A Novel
by Clemence McLaren

Clemence McLaren's novel presents the events of Homer's Odyssey *through the eyes of four female characters, Penelope, her servant Eurycleia, the witch Circe, and the goddess Athena.*

The First Olympic Athletes

BY JUDITH LLOYD YERO

In the days of legend, Zeus, the greatest of the Greek gods, hurled a lightning bolt from the top of **Mount Olympus**. It struck a place west of Athens. There, the Greeks built a great religious center— Olympia. It was dedicated to Zeus and the other gods. Olympia became the site of festivals filled with athletic competition, dance, and music—gifts of those same gods. The Olympic games were born.

Every four years, a messenger carried the announcement of the games from Elis, the location of Olympia, to all the Greek **city-states**.

People and Terms to Know

Mount Olympus (uh•LIHM•puhs)—highest point in Greece and the home of the Greek gods.

city-states—independent states each consisting of one city and its surrounding territory. A city-state included the free men and women who were born there, foreigners, and slaves.

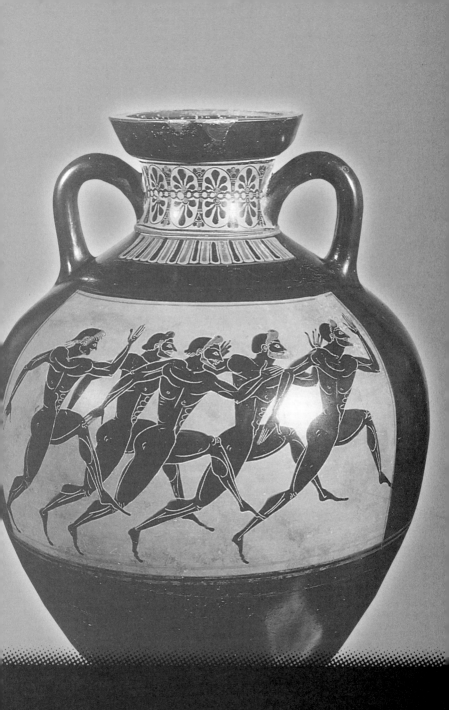

Greek runners are shown on a vase painting.

The messenger took with him a bronze **discus** listing the rules of the sacred **truce**. Even when the Greeks were engaged in serious wars, the fighting had to stop during the months surrounding the games. City-states that broke that agreement could not take part in the games. The truce was rarely broken.

Victory at the final competition was the highest honor a person could have.

Competition was of great importance in the education of young Greek men and women. It was considered the most sacred way to become perfect physically, spiritually, and intellectually. Victory at the final competition was the highest honor a person could have. It meant that his name would become immortal, that it would live forever.

Athletes trained for perfection. A young man who went on to victory in the games described an athlete's form:

People and Terms to Know

discus (DIHS·kuhs)—flat, circular plate or disk thrown for distance in athletic contests. The discus listing the rules was a special one.

truce (troos)—temporary halt in a war.

The neck should be upright like that of a horse which is beautiful and knows it. The . . . tops of the shoulders should be erect. A well-marked arm . . . must have broad veins starting from the neck, continuing to the throat, going down the shoulders and descending into the hands. The straight back is beautiful, but the slightly curved [back] is more athletic, in order to adapt to the bending and forward-leaning posture of wrestling. . . .

Above all, the proper athlete should have endurance, courage, and skill.

The Olympic games were organized and run by a group of judges. Dressed in their rich purple robes, they ruled the games with an iron fist. In order to provide the greatest spectacle, the judges supervised the athletes' training for a month before the games. They literally separated the men from the boys. In the earliest games, those who were beardless could not participate. Physical performance, overall character, and morality were the keys to selection by the judges.

And the judge has the whip at his disposal, not only for the athlete, but also for the trainer, and he uses it in case of any disobedience of his orders; and all have to conform with the orders of the judges, since those who violate them may be immediately thrown out of the games.

The Olympic festival was a sight to behold. Colorful tents along the banks of the river housed both athletes and spectators. Musicians and dancers entertained the crowds. Representatives of all the Greek city-states, dressed in their most colorful robes and riding in magnificent chariots, paraded through Olympia. Spectators crowded the hillside, straining to catch a glimpse of their favorite athlete or of some famous poet or politician. Although married women could not join the crowd, unmarried girls could.

Spectators crowded the hillside, straining to catch a glimpse of their favorite athlete.

The games began with a solemn sacrifice to Zeus. Then, the judges and athletes paraded from the **sanctuary** into the **stadium**. Spectators and athletes alike batted at the annoying flies, eager for the competition to begin. Standing proudly under the hot summer sun, the athletes had to swear that they were free-born Greeks of unmixed blood. They also swore that they would abide by the rules of the games, that they had obeyed the rules of diet and training for the last ten months, and that they had not committed any evil deed.

During the earliest games, the only competition was the *stade*—a race the length of the stadium. This was similar to the 200-meter race in the modern games.

Under the broiling sun, the athletes took their places at the starting line. With a loud blast of trumpets, the barriers fell, and the race was on. The runners stretched their long legs and pumped their arms, striving for victory. Only one runner could win, his name forever linked with the games in which the gods had favored him. On a day in 776 B.C., the first winner was recorded for all time. That man was Koroibos of Elis.

People and Terms to Know

sanctuary (SANGK•choo•EHR•ee)—sacred or holy place. At Olympia, it was a huge area made up of temples, altars, and other buildings.

stadium—large open area where the Olympic games were held. Grassy slopes where spectators could sit surrounded the stadium.

In later years, other sports were added to the games—longer running races, boxing, wrestling, and the **pentathlon**. The games expanded from a single day to five or more. The greatest moment of all was the final day.

As the sun set, the athletes again made their way to the temple of Zeus.

As the sun set, the athletes again made their way to the temple of Zeus. The crowds showered them with flowers and leaves. The winners carried palm branches and wore red wool strips around their heads—gifts from the judges when the event ended. In the temple, crowns of wild olive leaves lay on gold and ivory tables.

One by one the winners approached the temple. In the proudest moment of the athlete's life, his name, his father's name, and the name of his native city were announced to the crowd. The crown placed on his head proved that he was a favorite of the gods. The greatest honor was one of immortality, for winners had the right to erect statues of

People and Terms to Know

pentathlon (pehn•TATH•luhn)—athletic contest in which each participant competes in five track and field events.

themselves at Olympia, next to those of the gods who had supported their victories. Poems were written in the athletes' honor. Their names and the names of their cities were on everyone's lips.

The games ended with a great feast. The quiet valley of Olympia rang with the sounds of celebration, of singing, dancing, and praise for the greatest heroes of the games. And then, the games were over.

The names of the earliest Olympians did, indeed, become immortal. Even today, we tell their stories.

One wrestler won his events in six different Olympics over a period of 24 years. His strength was legendary. According to his people, he carried his own statue into Olympia after his victories gave him that right.

Another athlete won several Olympic events. It is said that when he was a boy of nine, he so admired a bronze statue of a god that he tore it from its base and took it home with him. Rather than being punished, he was made to carry it back. Because of his strength, his future at the games was assured.

A famous boxer won many victories, but he never struck any of his opponents. He believed that to injure someone else was to show a lack of bravery. Spectators enjoyed watching as he defended himself against the blows from his opponents without striking them. His opponents finally became so exhausted and so discouraged that they could no longer hit him. Then they gave up and admitted defeat.

In many ways, the spirit of those first Olympians still exists.

In many ways, the spirit of those first Olympians still exists in the men and women athletes of the modern games. In the words of a famous Greek poet,

But if, my heart, you wish to sing of contests,
look no further for any star warmer than the sun,
shining by day through the lonely sky, and let us
not proclaim any contest greater than Olympia.

QUESTIONS TO CONSIDER

1. In what ways were the early Olympics like the modern Olympics?

2. In what ways were the early Olympics not like the modern Olympics?

3. What is your opinion of the importance of competition in education today?

The Original Olympics
by Stewart Ross

Stewart Ross presents an account of the ancient Olympic games, a central event of Greek life for over 1,000 years.

Olympic Games in Ancient Greece
by Shirley Glubock and Alfred H. Tamarin

Shirley Glubock and Alfred H. Tamarin describe the Olympic games as they would have been around 400 B.C., when they were at their height.

The Story of the Olympics
by Dave Anderson (foreword by Carl Lewis)

Dave Anderson presents a history of the Olympics from its founding in 776 B.C. to the present.

Treating the Sick

BY STEPHEN CURRIE

Doctor Monacles (MAHN•uh•KLEEZ) squinted at the patient on the cot nearest the door, then turned to Tremolo and Cassia behind him. "We may as well begin here. Your complaint, sir?"

Cassia bit his lip. The patient's cheeks were pale, and sweat glistened on his forehead. *Probably has a fever,* Cassia told himself, his eyes scanning the man's face for other signs of distress. As he watched, the patient pressed one hand tightly against his eardrum.

"Earache," the patient whispered.

Monacles frowned as though he were looking at some unusual form of insect life. "Speak up."

The patient winced and tried again. "Earache," he murmured.

A Greek physician treats the shoulder of his patient in this ancient Greek carving.

A look of impatience crossed Monacles's face. "Eh?"

Cassia swallowed hard. He knew he was only supposed to observe. He was here in this hospital outside Athens to see how a master physician such as Monacles cared for patients. With luck, he knew, the great doctor would take him on as a student. It was not for Cassia himself to make remarks.

"Bleed him," he said.

Still, since Monacles seemed to be unable to hear the patient . . .

"He says he has an earache," Cassia explained shyly.

"Ah, an earache." Monacles straightened up. His lips curved into a satisfied smile. "Bleed him," he said.

"Bleed him," echoed Tremolo, Monacles's assistant, pulling a knife from a small box at his side.

"Bleed him?" repeated Cassia with a frown, watching as Tremolo sharpened the knife.

Monacles gave a long drawn-out sigh. "*Bleed* him," he said again, straightening up and directing the words at Cassia. "Bleeding is best for earaches. That and prayer." He turned to the patient again.

"Go to the temple, pray loudly for relief from . . ." He blinked and frowned. "From what was it?"

"Earaches," supplied Tremolo as he made a small cut in the patient's arm. "We'll do this every day until you're well again," he said as the blood began to flow.

Or until you die from loss of blood, whichever comes first, thought Cassia as Tremolo led the way to the next bed. To Cassia, the patient with the earache seemed to need something other than bloodletting. Gently he ran his hand across the man's forehead. He had a fever too. What was Doctor Monacles going to do about that? *Nothing,* he said to himself. Monacles hadn't even noticed.

Perhaps staying here in Athens was the wrong move. Monacles had a fine reputation in town, and Athens was certainly convenient. But Cassia still wasn't sure. He had heard about a doctor on the far-off island of **Kos,** a man with a hard name—Hippocalypse, Hippotanuse—no, **Hippocrates**, that was it.

People and Terms to Know

Kos (kahs)—island in the Aegean Sea off the southwest coast of ancient Ionia. See the map on page 12.

Hippocrates (hih•PAHK•ruh•TEEZ)—(c.460–c.377 B.C.) Greek doctor called "the Father of Medicine." The storyteller is telling a small joke. *Apocalypse* means the end of the world, and *hypotenuse* is one side of a right triangle.

Hippocrates was a forward-thinking physician. "The human body is a circle," Hippocrates had written. His meaning had been clear to Cassia. The body was a circle because every part was connected. You could not hope to heal unless you examined the whole body, the whole person, the whole soul.

"The human body is a circle," Hippocrates had written.

He frowned. Somehow, Doctor Monacles seemed not to understand that part.

"Well, he's almost cured," Monacles said, jutting out his chin with pride. "All it takes, my boy, is a fine doctor, like me. A doctor who can cure anyone, given enough time."

"Yes, sir," said Cassia dutifully, but he wondered. According to Hippocrates, bodies healed themselves. In his view, the physician was only a helper. If the man with the earache gets well, he asked himself, will it be because of Monacles, or because the man's own body cleansed itself?

He stepped to the next patient's bedside. This fellow was old and thin. His beard was tangled, and his sheets filthy. As Cassia watched, the man drew in a wheezing breath and then exploded in a series of hacking coughs. Soon, the man was doubled up, gasping for air.

"What's *your* trouble?" Monacles squinted down at the patient.

The man cannot breathe, Cassia thought impatiently. *Why ask when the answer is staring you in the face?*

H ippocrates would treat this man with care and compassion, he told himself. At least, according to everything he had heard about the doctor from Kos. "Where there is a love of medical arts," Hippocrates had written, "there is also a love of humanity." Cassia was not sure whether Monacles loved the medical arts, but he suspected the doctor did not have any great love for humanity.

It was a pity that Kos was so distant, he reflected with a sigh.

"Cannot—breathe," the patient husked, breaking into another series of coughs.

"A cough, I believe," Monacles said proudly. "A great doctor can always tell. Surgery is called for. Prepare the saw. Bleed him first, of course."

"Bleed him," echoed Tremolo, scurrying forward with the knife.

"Surgery?" Cassia stared at the physician. *Fresh air might help,* he thought. *Warm compresses on his chest could help too. Even a clean sheet might do some good—but surgery? What part would they cut?*

Hippocrates had something to say about that, too, Cassia recalled. He would say something about cures needing to connect to the complaint.

He'd talk about having an open and scientific mind. "Doctor Monacles," Cassia began.

The exact complaint did not seem to matter.

"Surgery is good for the sick," snapped Monacles. "Oh, and don't forget to pray, too. We'll be back in an hour to cut out the part that ails you, or some part anyhow. Next!"

Through the ward they hurried at breakneck speed. By the end of an hour, Cassia could have given Monacles's answers himself, and in his head he did just that, imitating the bored voice of the doctor. Bleed and cut. Cut and bleed. The exact complaint did not seem to matter. The cure was always the same.

"Ready?" asked Monacles, peering over the bedside of the man with the cough. His saw was in his hand.

"Ready," said Tremolo cheerfully, holding one of the man's arms tightly against the bed. Cassia bit his lip but held down the other arm, as he'd been told.

"Oh, please," whimpered the patient.

"Hush," suggested Monacles. "We have seven more to do. Time flies, you know." The man screamed, began to struggle, and suddenly jerked free.

"Pray," Monacles called, as the man, still coughing, disappeared out the door.

What had Hippocrates said? "Prayer indeed is good," Cassia quoted softly, "but while calling on the gods, a man should himself lend a hand."

A man should indeed, he thought, *and so should a doctor. A helpful hand.*

And in that instant Cassia made up his mind.

*   *   *

"Well, my boy," said Doctor Monacles later that day, "what do you think?" He draped a hand on Cassia's shoulder. Cassia shuddered. His hand was a little dirty. "You think too much for a lowly student, I fear. Still, I'll do you a favor and take you on. No need to thank me."

Cassia thought one last time of Monacles's one-cure-fits-all approach to healing, of his failure to think of patients as people. Then he thought of Hippocrates of Kos and his sense of **ethics**. He

---

People and Terms to Know

ethics—rules or standards of right and wrong for a person or the members of a profession.

believed that the patient was a whole person and a unique individual.

Somehow, traveling to Kos no longer seemed so impossible.

"No, thank you," he said, gently but firmly removing Monacles's hand from his shoulder.

QUESTIONS TO CONSIDER

1. Why did Cassia decide not to study medicine with Monacles?

2. In what ways did the medical treatments practiced by Monacles differ from treatments today?

3. What did Hippocrates have to say about the connection between the medical arts and humanity? What is your opinion about this?

4. What do you think Hippocrates meant when he said, "Prayer indeed is good, but while calling on the gods, a man should himself lend a hand"?

Greek Tradition

The Caduceus

The Greek god Hermes carried a staff called the caduceus (kuh•DOO•see•uhs). It had two serpents twining around it. The caduceus represented peace and symbolized Hermes's role as the messenger of the gods. A similar staff with one serpent around it was carried by Asclepius (uh•SKLEE•pee•uhs), the Greek god of healing. Because of this similarity, the caduceus of Hermes became the symbol of the modern medical profession.

How Would You Survive as an Ancient Greek?
by Fiona McDonald

Fiona McDonald explores what your life would have been like if you had been an ancient Greek. She describes what you ate, how you dressed, how you made a living, what you did for entertainment, what you believed, and what you did when you were sick.

Science in Ancient Greece
by Kathlyn Gay

Kathlyn Gay discusses the ideas and achievements of ancient Greek scientific thinkers such as Hippocrates.

Greek and Roman Science
by Don Nardo

Don Nardo examines the scientific ideas and practices of the ancient Greeks and Romans.

The Trial
of Socrates

BY DEE MASTERS

Anytus (an•EYE•tuhs) knew who was to blame for all the problems Athens had. It was **Socrates**.

After **Sparta** defeated Athens, the Spartans set up a government in Athens in which a few people held all the power. Democracy, of which the Athenians were so proud, disappeared. Now, although democracy was back, many Athenians were still angry. Socrates, a **philosopher**, had probably been on the side of those who had destroyed democracy, Anytus

---

People and Terms to Know

Socrates (SAHK•ruh•TEEZ)—(c. 470–399 B.C.) famous Greek philosopher who used a question-and-answer method of teaching. Although he left no writings, his ideas survived through the writings of Plato, one of his pupils.

Sparta—city-state of ancient Greece. It was famous for its soldiers. The Spartans defeated Athens in the Peloponnesian (PEHL•uh•puh•NEE•zhuhn) War (431–404 B.C.).

philosopher—seeker of truth. The Greek word *philosophos* means "lover of knowledge."

An ancient sculpture of Socrates.

thought. Oh, how he wanted to get rid of Socrates! But there was a problem. Socrates wasn't guilty of any crime.

Anytus persuaded a very religious young man, Meletus (meh•LEE•tuhs), to say that Socrates was guilty of not worshipping the official gods of the city. He believed in other gods, Meletus said. Socrates was also accused of poisoning the minds of young men with the ideas he taught them. These were very serious charges for which men had died in Athens.

In February 399 B.C., Socrates was put on trial on these charges. He was then 71 years old. He would be judged by 501 Athenian citizens.

In his defense, Socrates first had to clear up an old misunderstanding. He explained that "a long time ago, **Aristophanes** made fun of me in a play, *The Clouds.* The Socrates character in the play thought about the heavens and investigated things that were beneath the earth. He was good at using

---

People and Terms to Know

Aristophanes (AR•ih•STAHF•uh•neez)—(c. 448–c. 388 B.C.) Athenian comic playwright. *The Clouds* was written in 423 B.C.

tricky arguments. In the play, Aristophanes said that persons who study such things never believe in the gods. But, the truth is, Athenians, I have nothing to do with these matters. Has anyone ever heard me talk about such things?"

> "I would like to be able to educate men," Socrates answered. "But I don't know how."

No one really had.

Socrates turned to another part of the charge. Supposedly, he had been paid to teach young men and had misled them.

"I would like to be able to educate men," Socrates answered. "But I don't know how. So no one has ever paid me to do that."

And it was true. No one had ever paid him to teach.

"Well, what do you do?" asked one of the accusers.

Socrates paused before he spoke, "Many years ago a young man went to the **oracle of Delphi** and asked if any man was wiser than Socrates. The

---

People and Terms to Know

oracle (AWR•uh•kuhl) **of Delphi** (DEHL•fy)—shrine of the god Apollo in central Greece and the most sacred place in the Greek world. People went to Delphi to consult the priestess of Apollo, who revealed the god's answers to various questions. The answers were often puzzling.

priestess replied, 'No man is wiser than Socrates.' I was very upset because I knew I was not wise, but I also knew that the oracle of god did not lie.

"I searched for a truly wise man to explain the oracle to me. I went to the politicians, the poets, and the workers. Many thought they were wise, but when I asked them questions, it was clear they did not know what they thought they knew!

"I show men that they do not know what they think they know."

"I knew nothing. They knew nothing. My wisdom was to know that I didn't know anything.

"The oracle had given me a job. I show men that they do not know what they think they know. Perhaps then they can search for real wisdom."

Then Socrates called on the man who had accused him. "Meletus, do you mean I teach young men to believe in other gods or that I do not believe in any gods?"

Hoping to make Socrates look as bad as possible, Meletus answered, "I mean you do not believe in any gods."

"Do you mean that I do not believe the sun and moon to be gods as our religion says they are?" asked Socrates.

Now the truth was that almost no one believed that anymore, so some people laughed when Meletus answered, "He does not believe! He says the sun is a stone, and the moon is dirt!"

"Friend, Meletus," Socrates said, "you have me confused with someone else. I have not said those things."

And he hadn't.

"You do not believe in the gods!" Meletus shouted.

Socrates quickly answered, "When you accused me, you said that I believed in other gods. Now you say I don't believe in any gods. You contradict yourself.

"Fellow Athenians, it seems that Meletus is a very proud young man who is confused."

Which, of course, was true.

Socrates continued, "I have always done what I thought right. I am not afraid of death. Three times I fought for Athens. I went where my commander sent me. The gods have sent me here. I will stay here doing what the gods ask. I will not change my ways. I will not stop hunting for the truth. I will keep asking questions.

"The gods have sent me to be the gadfly that bothers the great horse of the government. All governments need someone to bother and question them. If you kill me, you will not find me easy to replace. I do believe there are gods, and to them and to you I turn over my case."

After Socrates finished speaking, the jury voted. The vote was guilty, 281 to 220. The majority thought that questioning the government was bad, so Socrates was dangerous.

Meletus asked for the death penalty. No one thought the old man would really be put to death. They would just send him somewhere else, to ask other people his bothersome questions.

Socrates addressed the jury, "I am not upset, Athenians. I am surprised. I thought there would be more votes against me. If I ask to be sent away and not allowed to return, you will probably do that. Then I would be admitting that I am guilty. I am not guilty. So I will ask for what I deserve.

"Instead of gaining wealth, I have tried to help every man see that he must look at himself and seek goodness and wisdom. I tell you there is nothing better for a man and his city than for him to discuss goodness and question his own beliefs. The unexamined life is not worth living.

"The unexamined life is not worth living."

"What do I deserve? I suggest you give me free meals for the rest of my life."

The jury was angry! Socrates was making fun of the trial. The jury delivered a death sentence.

Socrates rose to speak a last time. "You will get rid of one old man. You could have waited. I will not be around to bother Athens much longer. Now your enemies will say that Athens has killed a wise old man, whether I am wise or not.

"I am innocent. I refuse to do wrong to save my life. I think it is much harder to escape from evil than from death. Evil is faster than death. Old and slow, Socrates has been caught by death. You who are smart and fast have been caught by evil.

"Sadly, for you, I will not be quiet even in death. Others will remember what I say and what you do.

There is a small voice inside of me that tells me when something is evil. It has not told me that what I am doing is evil.

"I feel that death is either an eternal sleep, a peaceful rest, which sounds good to an old man, or death is a journey. I will go where all the great men have gone. Perhaps I will have a chance to question them.

"We go different ways now. I go to die. You go to live. Only the gods know which is better."

And he went.

QUESTIONS TO CONSIDER

1. What were the charges against Socrates?

2. What did Socrates mean when he said he was "the gadfly that bothers the great horse of government"?

3. Why didn't Socrates ask for a lesser punishment?

4. If you had been one of the citizens judging Socrates, how would you have voted?

Creating Empires

Interview with a Spartan

BY WALTER HAZEN

I was not surprised to find Zethos in perfect health.
Even at the age of 60, his body was trim and his
muscles as firm as ropes. And why shouldn't they
be? He had spent his entire life in the army. He had
trained hard, he had fought hard, and he had lived a
life free of all luxuries. He had not been retired long
enough for his body to grow soft and lazy.

Let me introduce myself. My name is
Alexandros, and I have come to Zethos's farm outside the city of Sparta to talk to him about his life in
the army. At first, he didn't want to answer my
questions. He told me that Spartan soldiers were
expected to remain silent at all times. They were
only to speak when spoken to, and then their
remarks had to be brief. He finally opened up when
I reminded him that he was no longer in the army.

This bronze sculpture of a Greek warrior dates from the 6th century B.C.

"Where do you want to begin?" he asked.

"Start when you were seven and you left home to begin your army training," I answered.

Zethos sighed and began his story. He said that his leaving home meant that his parents had no children in the house. His baby sister, Cassandra, had been taken away by soldiers shortly after she was born. Like all Spartan babies who are not in perfect health, she was taken to the mountains and left to die. His older brother, Priamos, had been killed several years earlier fighting the Persians at the Battle of **Thermopylae**. His parents accepted such sad things. They were natural.

"I remember mother telling him to come back either with his shield, or on it."

"Was your mother proud of Priamos?" I asked.

"Of course," he replied. He seemed surprised by my question. "I remember mother telling him to come back either with his shield, or on it. She was proud that he died a brave soldier. She was even more proud that he died fighting alongside King **Leonidas**."

People and Terms to Know

Thermopylae (thuhr•MAHP•uh•lee)—narrow pass through mountains in east-central Greece. It was the site of an unsuccessful Spartan stand against the Persians in 480 B.C.

Leonidas (lee•AHN•ih•duhs)—(died 480 B.C.) Spartan king who led a small force against a huge Persian army at Thermopylae. All the Spartans were killed.

"Suppose your little sister Cassandra had been allowed to live," I continued. "What would have been expected of her?"

Again, Zethos seemed surprised that I would ask, what was to him, such a silly question.

"Why, she would have participated in outdoor games and kept herself physically fit. Then she would have married and had lots of babies for the glory of Sparta."

Zethos continued his story. After being taken from his home, he lived in army housing with others. There he was assigned to a group of boys. Each group was led by an older and stronger boy referred to as a "captain." Captains were very strict and took special delight in making life miserable for those in their charge.

"We were punched, kicked, and publicly whipped," Zethos explained. "And one dared not whine or complain. To show evidence of pain only brought more punishment."

From the start, Zethos was given only enough food to stay alive. Part of his training was to learn to steal food. Stealing was permitted and encouraged, but if a boy was caught, he was severely punished.

"I heard of one boy," Zethos continued, "who was so hungry he stole a fox to eat. A trainer came upon him with the fox. To avoid being caught, the boy hid the animal under his cloak. While he was being questioned by the trainer, he kept the fox hidden away. He never made a sound or cried out as the fox scratched and gnawed at his side. Finally he collapsed and died. Or at least that's the way the story went."

Zethos said that the starvation diet helped teach him discipline and toughness. The clothing he wore did the same. Both summer and winter he was allowed only a simple cloak. He wore no shoes, going barefoot in even the worst of weather. At night, he slept in his cloak on a hard bed made of the stems of plants.

"Good old **Lycurgus**," Zethos said, smiling. "He certainly made things hard for me."

People and Terms to Know

Lycurgus (ly•KUR•guhs)—Spartan lawmaker who lived in the 800s B.C.

I agreed. Lycurgus had drawn up laws that controlled everything about Spartan life. His laws turned Sparta into a **military dictatorship**. He had no use whatever for democracy.

Zethos continued his story. He said that he was in training for about twelve years. When he was 20, he became a soldier and he remained a soldier until the age of 60. He was allowed to marry when he was 20, but he had to continue living with other soldiers until he was 30. After that, he could live at home with his wife. Even then, he continued to eat his meals with his fellow soldiers at an army mess hall.

His laws turned Sparta into a military dictatorship.

"How were the meals in the mess hall?" I asked him.

"Nothing to rave about," he replied, again smiling. "Mostly black broth and bread. Maybe a little wine. Once a week, ordinary citizens ate in a similar dining hall. The reason for this was to keep them tough too. If you weren't tough in Sparta, you didn't make it.

People and Terms to Know

military dictatorship—type of government in which the armed forces have complete control.

"Oh, I'll tell you how bad the food was at those public dining halls. A visitor who had eaten at one was supposed to have said afterward: 'Now I know why the Spartans do not fear death!' I think that just about sums it up."

When Zethos told me that citizens had to supply part of what they ate at the dining hall, I naturally wondered what happened if they could not come up with their share.

"Why, they lost all their rights as citizens," he said, once again surprised that I would ask a question whose answer to him was quite obvious.

I concluded my interview with Zethos when I asked him about his battlefield experiences. Having been too young for the Persian Wars, he said that most of his fighting was confined to putting down revolts of the **helots.** But from that, he wore battle scars of which he was very proud.

People and Terms to Know

helots (HEHL•uhts)—people in Sparta who were neither slave nor free but farmed the estates of citizens. They could own property of their own, however. Since they outnumbered the citizens, they had to be kept from rebelling.

Zethos excused himself, saying it was time for his morning exercise. Even at his age, he was determined to remain fit and trim as long as possible.

Once a Spartan, always a Spartan!

QUESTIONS TO CONSIDER

1. Why was Zethos at first reluctant to give an interview?

2. What is your opinion about the training of young Spartans?

3. How would you explain the comment of the visitor to the mess hall of the Spartans?

4. How would you have reacted to life in Sparta?

Women of Sparta

The Spartan Lycurgus wanted the young women of Sparta to be strong and better able to bear children. Spartan girls wrestled, ran and threw spears. They also participated in solemn feasts where they would sing songs praising brave warriors.

Their education taught young Spartan women simplicity and a care for good health,  and gave them some taste of higher feelings, admitted as they thus were to the field of noble action and glory. . . . Some foreign lady told [Gorgo, the wife of a Spartan king] that the women of Sparta were the only women in the world who could rule men. "With good reason," Gorgo said, "for we are the only women who give birth to men."

—Plutarch, *Life of Lycurgus*

▲
This carving is from the grave of the daughter of a Spartan king.

Explorer from the Future

BY BARBARA LITTMAN

Oh, this doesn't get easier. My fourth time jump, and I still feel like my stomach is in my head.

But, I'm here. Thank goodness the Jump Masters figured out how to make me invisible. Until they did, it looked like Joe was going to do the history check on Athens and the **Peloponnesian War**. Everyone knew I was the expert, but no way could a visible woman jump to 432 B.C. and fit in.

Well, the Jump Masters were right. I landed just behind the **agora**. Let me check my Jump Handler.

People and Terms to Know

Peloponnesian (PEHL•uh•puh•NEE•zhun) **War**—war between Athens and Sparta from 431 to 404 B.C.

agora (AG•uhr•uh)—ancient Greek marketplace.

During the time of Pericles, beautiful temples and monuments such as the Parthenon (upper right) were built on the Acropolis of Athens.

Pericles should be just about ready to give his famous speech about war with Sparta. I'll figure out where the assembly is held.

There's a wonderful smell! It must be market day. If only I were able to eat. I could try some real Greek olive oil and goat's cheese. And the fish look fresher than anything I'd find from a gro-tub in 2089. And those jugs the women are filling at the fountain are beautiful beyond description. We know that under Pericles there was a

Under Pericles there was a Golden Age of Greek art.

Golden Age of Greek art. If these simple jars are any example, I can't wait to get to the **Acropolis** and see the buildings and sculpture.

I've already been to Sparta. How different Sparta and Athens are! In Athens, men stroll through the agora discussing philosophy. In Sparta, I was surrounded by boys and young men boxing and practicing their fighting skills in unarmed combat.

People and Terms to Know

Pericles (PEHR•ih•KLEEZ)—(c. 500–429 B.C.) Athenian statesman and general known for his speeches, his building program, and his democratic reforms. The period 460–429 B.C. is sometimes called the Periclean Age or the Golden Age of Athens. He led the Athenians in the opening battle of the Peloponnesian Wars.

Acropolis (uh•KRAHP•uh•lihs)—high fortified place in Athens on which the Parthenon was built. In ancient Greek cities, the acropolis would be the safest place when enemies attacked.

Well, I'd always read that Spartan boys were raised to be warriors, taken from their homes at the age of seven to begin military training. It was also surprising to see so many women and girls about. Some were even hanging around the boys as they fought, egging them on and teasing the losers. It was very different in Athens. You would think that in a democracy like Athens where liberty is so highly prized, women would have the right to mingle in public like they do in Sparta. In Athens, though, all but the poorest women and girls are kept inside, away from the peering eyes of men. How small their lives must be compared to mine—or even to the women of Sparta.

Sparta *looks* different from Athens too. Large buildings like the ones in Athens are nowhere to be seen. Sparta's buildings are not unattractive. They just aren't great. Also, I didn't see even one foreigner wandering among the crowds. Well, that's Sparta's loss. Athens has gained much from its contact with people from other countries. They are welcomed by Pericles.

I want to get up to the Acropolis before Pericles's speech. I can't wait to get inside the **Parthenon** and

---

People and Terms to Know

Parthenon (PAHR•thuh•NAHN)—temple of Athena built on the Acropolis.

see the sculpture of Athena. If it hadn't been for Pericles, the Acropolis would be in ruins. The Persians really did a number on it during the war. Pericles convinced the assembly that the Parthenon and other temples should be rebuilt at public expense.

Even though I'm not visible, I'm tired. Since no one can see me, I'm going to sleep right here at Athena's feet.

*　　*　　*

Oh no, I slept too long. I've got to get down to the agora right away. I can't miss Pericles's speech to the assembly. They're starting to gather. There are only men there, of course. Thank goodness no one can see me. Only the free, adult men can participate in Athens's democracy. Women and slaves are excluded. Of course, how different is that from the beginnings of my democracy? American slaves were property, not people, according to the laws of the time. Women couldn't vote in national elections until 1920!

Only the free, adult men can participate in Athens's democracy.

Pericles is certainly impressive. Everyone is nervously waiting for him to speak. (I know he will recommend war, but they don't.) I can see their respect for this man, who has guided Athens for almost 30 years. He has strengthened its democracy while serving as Athens's most influential general. One of his best ideas was to pay citizens who serve on juries and in public offices. That way not just wealthy people can participate in democracy. (We do that now, over three thousand years later.)

Oh, here, he's beginning.

"It was evident before that Sparta was plotting against us, and now it is even more evident."

An ancient sculpture of Pericles. ▶

Jump Report

From: Susan

To: Director of Historic Truth

Date: May 9, 2089

Subject: Athens 432 B.C.

Pericles just recommended war to the assembly. Before his speech, I jumped to Sparta and witnessed the Spartan assembly doing the same. It is just as **Thucydides** reports in his *History of the Peloponnesian War.*

After his speech, Pericles recommended that all people and animals be brought inside the walls of the city for protection. My next jump will be into the future at Athens to hear Pericles's famous funeral speech honoring the soldiers who died in the war. I know the town will be crowded and **plague**-ridden by then. It will be a sad sight.

Everyday life in both Athens and Sparta seems just as our records report.

People and Terms to Know

Thucydides (thoo•SIHD•ih•DEEZ)—(c.460–c.400 B.C.) Greek historian considered the greatest historian of ancient times.

plague (playg)—very dangerous disease that spreads rapidly and often causes death. The term *plague-ridden* means "full of the plague."

*   *   *

I will return after his speech; the Jump Masters have warned that I may not be able to become visible again if I wait too long.

Whew! Another jump! I'm late. I can see the procession already outside the city gates. It has almost reached the large tent where the bones of the dead and offerings lie. The coffins are beautiful, handmade from cypress wood. So many people are following the wagons. Mothers of the dead are weeping and crying out.

Pericles is on a high platform, looking out over the mourning crowd. His voice is strong, but I can hear the sorrow in it. As Thucydides reports, he is encouraging the crowd and praising Athens's many great deeds. He is offering comfort to the survivors of the dead.

People are returning to the city now. What a sad procession.

I cannot stay another second—I could become permanently invisible at any moment.

Final Jump Report Filed After Return to 2089

From: Susan

To: Director of Historic Truth

Date: May 13, 2089

Subject: Athens 431 B.C.

By the time Pericles made his famous funeral speech, Athens was overcrowded beyond belief. Food supplies were low, and bodies of plague victims were piled in corners, waiting to be burned or buried.

We know Pericles was blamed for the plague and removed from office as a result. Though he was made leader again, he died shortly afterward from the plague.

Food supplies were low, and bodies of plague victims were piled in corners.

I recommend another jump to the period. We cannot learn too much from this man. His ideas were far ahead of his time. It is important to remember that, after Pericles's democracy, there was not another democracy for over 1,000 years.

QUESTIONS TO CONSIDER

1. Who was Pericles?

2. What are two things that Pericles was famous for?

3. What are some differences between Athens and Sparta?

4. How was the democracy of Athens different from the democracy of the United States today?

Funeral Speech of Pericles

The Greek historian Thucydides recorded the famous speech that Pericles gave in honor of the Athenian soldiers who had died in the war with Sparta.

So died these men as became Athenians. You, their survivors, must determine to have as firm a purpose in battle, though you may pray to have a happier result. . . .

You must realize the power of Athens, and feed your eyes upon her from day to day, till love of her fills your hearts; and then when all her greatness shall break upon you, you must reflect that it was by courage, sense of duty, and a keen feeling of honor in action that men were enabled to win all this, and that no personal failure in an enterprise could make them consent to deprive their country of their courage, but they laid it at her feet as the most glorious contribution they could offer.

—Thucydides,
The History of the Peloponnesian War

Alexander the Great Tames His Horse

BY LYNNETTE BRENT

"Elias, go and groom the horse one more time. I want him to look wonderful. We will be asking King Philip a very high price for this stallion."

I hurried to the stable to collect my grooming supplies. Philonicus (fih•LAWN•uh•kuhs) was eager to impress the king. This horse was a real prize. King **Philip** would be proud to have such a strong animal. If Philonicus were able to sell this horse, he would be a wealthy man.

People and Terms to Know

Philip—(382–336 B.C.) Philip II, king of Macedonia in northern Greece from 359 to 336 B.C. He was a brilliant general who conquered Greek city-states to the south and left an empire for his son Alexander to build on.

This ancient mosaic shows Alexander on his horse Bucephalus at the battle of Issus, where he defeated the king of Persia in 333 B.C.

I walked the horse into the sunny field. I went over the horse's coat with a stiff brush. His coat was a silky black, and the sunlight made it gleam. On the stallion's forehead was a white mark that looked like a flame. I would miss this horse once he was sold. I spoke softly to him as I brushed his white forehead. I told him that we would travel to the palace later in the day.

On the stallion's forehead was a white mark that looked like a flame.

Philonicus called out to me, "Where are you, Elias?"

I brought the horse back around to the stable. Philonicus was waiting for us.

"It is time to go. I don't want to be late for our appointment with King Philip." Philonicus was already upon his horse. I tied the lead of the black stallion to Philonicus's horse. Then I followed them to the palace.

Along the roads that led to the palace, I noticed a party of wealthy travelers. Horses were carrying beautiful cloth that was used for tents. One of the men in the traveling party was reciting poetry. Another was playing a lute, a small stringed instrument. Slaves followed, carrying their belongings in baskets. They were carrying enough supplies for a short trip. I wondered out loud where they might have been. Philonicus explained that they were most likely on their way home from the games held in Olympia.

At the palace, I took a small brush out of my bag to clean up the stallion before we saw the king. I cleaned the dust from his coat and then led the horse to the field behind the stable where King Philip was waiting. The huge building cast a shadow on the field. After the long journey, I was glad to be out of the hot sun.

Philonicus was already talking to King Philip and a member of his **cavalry**. I heard Philonicus mention a price of 13 **talents**. I was so shocked by the amount that he was asking that I gasped. I looked around quickly to see if anyone noticed. It was my job to stay in the background and not be noticed. The only person who seemed to hear me was Philip's son, **Alexander**.

People and Terms to Know

cavalry (KAV•uhl•ree)—troops trained to fight on horseback.

talents—unit of money used in ancient Greece, Rome, and the Middle East. A Greek talent was equal to about 58 pounds of a precious metal, such as silver or gold.

Alexander—(356–323 B.C.) known as Alexander III and "Alexander the Great." He was king of Macedonia from 336 to 323 B.C.

Alexander looked to be about 13 years old. His skin was fair, but his cheeks were flushed, as if he had been running. He looked at me as if he were amused by my slip. I hoped that he would not mention my mistake to Philonicus. I watched Alexander as he walked near his father.

Alexander had quite a reputation.

Alexander had quite a reputation. He was talented. He could recite poetry, act, play music, and hunt as well as any man in King Philip's court. He was experienced in matters of diplomacy. Why, at the age of six he met with Persian ambassadors when his father was away! His parents were so impressed with his intelligence that they hired **Aristotle** himself to become the boy's tutor. Aristotle traveled all the way from Athens to become Alexander's teacher. Now, Alexander was a student of politics and philosophy. He was well on his way to becoming a great leader.

People and Terms to Know

Aristotle (AR•ih•STAHT•uhl)—(384–322 B.C.) famous ancient Greek philosopher. Born in Macedonia, he went to Athens to study with Plato. He returned to Macedonia to tutor Alexander.

As I led the stallion to the field, I hoped that Alexander would keep my mistake to himself. Quickly, my concern for myself changed to concern for the horse. The calm, obedient stallion that I knew was now very restless. I had to drag the horse into the field with all my might. It was as if I were leading a wild, untamed horse.

The commotion with the stallion drew the attention of King Philip and Philonicus. King Philip sent his best rider to try out the horse. Instead of riding, the horseman was thrown into the air and onto the ground. The horse was getting more and more out of control.

The king dismissed Philonicus and our beautiful horse. As we pulled him out of the field, we passed young Alexander. I held my breath, hoping he wouldn't say anything about me to Philonicus. He started to speak, and I was surprised by what he said.

Alexander was trying to speak to the king. Even the king's son shouldn't speak directly to the king. It was so unusual, nobody paid attention to him at first. But Alexander became louder and louder until he had everyone's attention.

King Philip turned to Alexander. He was clearly offended. Yet his son refused to be silent. Finally, Philip agreed to listen. Alexander demanded a chance to ride the horse and keep it for himself. King Philip was trying not to laugh. If the cavalry's best horseman couldn't ride the horse, how could the boy do it? Alexander's answer? If he tried and failed, he would pay the 13 talents himself.

If the cavalry's best horseman couldn't ride the horse, how could the boy do it?

This time I was not the only one to gasp. Thirteen talents is an enormous amount of silver or gold! Most men can work their whole lives and not have that much money.

I was not surprised that the king took him up on the challenge. When Alexander failed at riding the horse, he would learn his place. This would certainly be the last time that he spoke so boldly and rudely to the king.

Alexander came over and took the horse's lead. "What is the horse's name?" he asked.

"His name is **Bucephalus**," I replied.

Alexander nodded, but did not try to mount him right away. Instead, he led the horse into a different part of the field. He whispered to him the entire time. None of us dared to speak. Was the stallion really returning to his right mind? He seemed quiet, but we held our breath as Alexander climbed onto the horse's back. We were sure that the horse would throw him. I hoped that the king's doctor was nearby.

Amazingly enough, the stallion not only allowed Alexander to ride, he seemed to enjoy the exercise. After a short trot around the field, Alexander confidently climbed down and approached the king.

"How did you do it?" I asked. Immediately I knew I should not have spoken, but I couldn't help it. Luckily, everyone was asking the same question, and no one noticed that I had spoken out of turn.

Alexander explained that he had begun to notice that the horse acted scared as soon as we

People and Terms to Know

Bucephalus (byoo•SEHF•uh•luhs)—Alexander the Great's war horse. The name means "ox-headed."

walked into the shaded area of the field. He had watched the stallion as we approached the palace and had decided that the horse must be frightened by the shadows. Alexander was able to calm the horse simply by walking him into the sun where the shadows would be behind him. Once he was out in the sun, the stallion was back to being the horse that I had groomed so carefully this morning. I would miss him, but I knew that Alexander would treat him well.

His son had shown himself to be wise beyond his years.

King Philip was beaming with pride. His son had shown himself to be wise beyond his years. Philip then announced that Alexander would have to go out and find a kingdom equal to his worth. Ours was too small for a man as brilliant as Alexander!

QUESTIONS TO CONSIDER

1. What does this story tell you about family life in ancient Greece?

2. What does the story tell you about the life of a servant?

3. In your opinion, what qualities did Alexander have as a young man that would eventually make him a leader?

Alexander's Empire

By the time he died in 323 B.C. at the age of 33, Alexander had conquered a huge empire. It stretched from Macedonia to the borders of India. (See the map below.) Alexander built more than 70 new cities in his empire. He named at least a dozen for himself, including Alexandrias in Egypt, Persia, and Bactria. When Alexander was invading India, his horse Buchephalus died. To honor him, Alexander established the city of Bucephalia there.

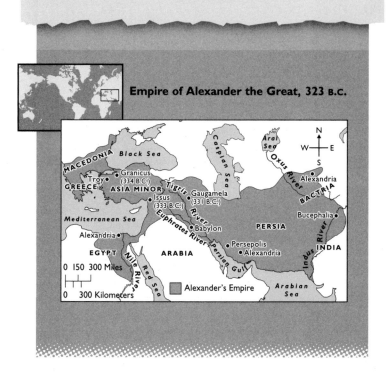

Empire of Alexander the Great, 323 B.C.

Alexander the Great
by Robert Green

Robert Green's biography introduces the life and achievements of Alexander the Great.

The World in the Time of Alexander the Great
by Fiona McDonald

Fiona McDonald presents the story of Alexander the Great and examines what was happening in the rest of the world during his lifetime.

Alexander the Great
by Maureen Ash

Maureen Ash's biography of Alexander emphasizes his role as an explorer.

Art, Architecture, and Literature

Aesop's Wonderful Fables

BY SHARON FRANKLIN

There was once an inexperienced and fearful storyteller. He was invited to practice telling stories in front of a group of children to increase his confidence. As he looked nervously out at his audience, he wondered why they would choose to listen to him. He wasn't a good storyteller, of that he was certain. With a sigh he began to speak.

"Today I will tell three of the fables of **Aesop.** The first one has both animal and human characters. Oh dear, now please don't go!" he said, wringing his hands. "I'll give you each a coin to listen!"

People and Terms to Know

Aesop (EE•sahp)—Greek storyteller who lived about 500 B.C. Fables are intended to teach a lesson or show some truth.

ESOPVS

This illustration of Aesop was created in the Middle Ages. It shows him surrounded by images illustrating his fables. His name appears above him

The children agreed. No one moved as he began to tell the fable.

The Man, His Son, and the Donkey

One day a man and his son were taking their donkey to market. They passed a group of young men who laughed at the sight of the man and his son walking along. "How silly you are!" they cried. "Why are you walking when you have a donkey to carry you?"

The man put his son on the donkey, and they went on their way. Soon a group of old women passed by. They clucked at the sight of the son riding on the donkey. "Shame on you, lazy boy. How can you ride when your poor father has to walk?"

The boy got down from the donkey and helped his father up. They went along in this way until they passed two men.

"How dare you let your poor son walk while you ride," they said. The man helped his son on so they were both riding.

Soon they passed a farmer who looked at them and laughed. "How can you ride that poor donkey? He will be so hot and tired that no one will want to buy him."

The man and his son did the only thing left to do. They got two poles and tied the donkey's legs to them. They put the poles on their shoulders and continued on, carrying the donkey upside down between them.

When they reached the market, the towns-people saw the man and boy carrying the donkey. They roared with laughter. The man and his son became so angry that they dropped the poles—and the donkey—to the ground with a great thud. With that the ties broke, and the donkey ran off, never to be seen again.

The man and his son did the only thing left to do.

The man and his son sadly headed for home. It had been a very bad day. In trying to please everyone, they hadn't pleased anyone, including themselves.

*　*　*

"In that story the main characters were two people who caused their own problems. My next fable's main characters are animals—a clever fox and a too-trusting goat. Please, now! I'll give you each a toy if you will stay and listen."

The children looked at each other. How could they refuse? No one moved.

The Fox and the Goat

Once upon a time there was a fox who, in a fit of thirst, leaned too far over a well. Alas, she fell in, right to the bottom, where she landed with a splash. The well was deep, and she could not climb out again.

After a time, a goat happened by and heard loud noises coming from the well. The day was warm, and the goat was thirsty as well as curious. He put his front legs over the edge and leaned over. He peered down the well and saw the fox.

"Well, well, my friend," said the goat cheerfully. "How's the water in that well? Is it fit to drink?"

The fox replied, "Never better. It is the sweetest, coldest, most delicious water I've ever had the pleasure to drink on such a hot day. I'd be happy to share it with you. Why don't you join me?"

Aesop listens to the fox, from an ancient Greek vase painting. ▶

The goat, perhaps too thirsty to think, jumped in and landed, *kerplunk,* right beside the fox. The fox welcomed the goat, and they sat together, drinking water and having a pleasant conversation. When the sun was setting and it began to get dark, however, the goat became worried about how to get out.

"Don't worry," said the fox. "I know just what to do. First, you stand up very tall, keeping your head nice and straight. I'll climb on your back, then up onto your head, and finally onto your beautiful horns in order to reach the top of the well. Once I've climbed out, I'll lean over and pull you up."

"Next time make sure you have a good way out before you jump in over your head."

The goat thought this was a splendid idea. He stood up as straight and tall as he could so the fox could climb on his back.

The fox sprang up onto the goat's back and then onto his horns. Finally, with a quick bounce she bounded up and out of the well, leaving the goat stuck at the bottom, surrounded by nothing but water.

As the fox ran off, laughing merrily, she shouted, "You silly goat. Next time make sure you have a good way out before you jump in over your head."

*   *   *

"Some of Aesop's fables are well known, like this last story I will tell you. At the end, see if you can state the moral. Oh my goodness," he added nervously, "I almost forgot, I have a piece of cake for anyone who stays."

Not one child moved.

The Boy Who Cried "Wolf!"

There was a young shepherd boy who tended his flock of sheep on a hill near a village. Sometimes he would get just a tiny bit lonely and a tiny bit bored. Then, just for a little fun, he liked to fool the people in the village into thinking a wolf was attacking his sheep. To do this, he simply cried, "Wolf! Wolf!" The villagers, certain that something was wrong, would come running to help the boy protect his flock. When they arrived, they usually found him lying in the shade, laughing at his clever trick. The villagers would return to their chores, shaking their heads and grumbling.

One afternoon while the boy was in the pasture with his flock, he saw something out of the corner of his eye. It was a real wolf! Frightened, he cupped his hands to his mouth and cried "Wolf! Wolf!" as loudly as he could, over and over.

The villagers heard his cries. But, they had heard them too many times before. Certain that they were being fooled once again, they continued on with their work, ignoring the boy's cries for help. As for the wolf, he did what wolves do—he killed every sheep in the flock.

* * *

When the storyteller finished, the children remained seated. "Why are you sitting here? I have no more treats for you. Good-bye." He turned away, looking quite sad, and put on his coat. It was then that one child came up and tugged at the storyteller's coat.

"Sir, thank you for the treats, but you don't have to bribe us. We love your stories. Can you tell us another one?"

And so it was in this way that the storyteller learned an important lesson of his own.

QUESTIONS TO CONSIDER

1. Why were fables a good way to speak your mind in an age when free speech was not allowed?

2. Why does "trying to please everyone" sometimes result in problems for a person?

3. What "lesson" was learned by the storyteller?

Aesop's Fables
by Jerry Pinkney

Jerry Pinkney gathers, retells, and illustrates more than sixty of Aesop's fables.

A Sip of Aesop
by Jane Yolen

Jane Yolen retells in verse thirteen of Aesop's fables, including "The Boy Who Cried Wolf."

I Was Once a Monkey: Stories Buddha Told
by Jeanne M. Lee

Many other cultures used fables to teach lessons. Jeanne M. Lee retells a group of the Indian fables known as Jataka tales. These tales were originally told by the Buddha to his followers to illustrate how they should treat others. The Jataka tales feature animal characters, which are often the Buddha himself in one of his previous lives.

The Mystery of Phidias

BY JUDY VOLEM

"**D**o you think he did it? Did he really steal the gold that covered the very statue he created? What happened to him?"

I waited impatiently for my grandfather to answer. He had told me a story of jealousy and mystery, and now he left me wondering as he filled his pipe.

My grandfather was an archaeologist, and he had taken me to see the place he was working on in the Acropolis in the middle of ancient Athens. We walked through a grove of fragrant orange trees and up a steep, well-worn path crowded with tourists. As we passed through the massive entrance, we saw the worn columns of the Parthenon rising above the remains of other temples. I was surprised to see piles

This is a modern artist's idea of how Phidias's statue must have looked.

of huge marble blocks scattered about as if a giant had thrown a fit.

"You have to use your deepest imagination," my grandfather said. "There was a time, over 2,000 years ago, when all of these temples were new. Their gleaming white marble was covered with gloriously painted carvings.

"No one could match his ability to create images of the gods with such majesty and precision."

"Imagine a magnificent bronze statue of the goddess Athena standing out in the open. She was so tall that her spear was visible to ships in the harbor. Another enormous statue of Athena stood inside the Parthenon. She brought much honor to her creator, **Phidias**, but she brought him trouble as well."

This was part of the mystery that my grandfather told me as we rested in the shade of a large column.

"Phidias was known throughout ancient Greece as the best sculptor by far. No one could match his ability to create images of the gods with such majesty and precision. For his great skills, he was chosen by Pericles to oversee the construction of the Parthenon.

People and Terms to Know

Phidias (FIHD•ee•uhs)—(c. 500–c. 432 B.C.) Athenian sculptor considered the greatest artist of ancient Greece.

Phidias directed the **architects** who designed the building and the workers who built and decorated it.

"It was a great time for Athens. Pericles had beaten the city's enemies in battle, and the people of Athens felt confident and powerful. With their agreement, Pericles decided that great monuments should be built on the Acropolis. Magnificent temples would show off the greatness of Athens and honor the gods as well.

"Work began on the Parthenon in 447 B.C. Men who had been soldiers labored on the construction of the temples during peacetime. They cut blocks of marble from a mountain ten miles from the Acropolis. Using ox-drawn carts, they hauled tons of marble across steep and dangerous country.

"Strength was not the only skill required. Architects made detailed mathematical calculations to build the tall columns. Talented sculptors carved the panels above the columns, showing stories of famous battles and processions. Skilled artists added ivory and bronze to the scenes. Colored glass and bright paint decorated the sculptures. The temple shone with movement and color.

People and Terms to Know

architects (AHR•kih•tehkts)—designers of buildings and other large structures.

"Imagine that," my grandfather repeated as we gazed upon the golden marble ruins before us now. "And now, picture Phidias, supervising the entire project that was completed in only about 15 years.

"Even as the Parthenon was being built, Phidias worked on his masterpiece. It was Athena, the goddess honored by Athenians as their guardian. The statue stood nearly 40 feet tall. Her face, hands, and feet were covered with ivory. Precious gems sparkled in her eyes. Dressed in a golden tunic that reached to her feet, Athena carried a statue of Victory in one hand and her spear in the other. A shield covered with carvings showing the Greeks fighting the Amazons was placed at her feet. A serpent rose up by her side. Even her helmet was carved with figures from mythology. She was precious beyond words. It was said that Phidias's extraordinary imagination created a vision of Athena never seen before.

Athena carried a statue of Victory in one hand and her spear in the other.

"Phidias had every right to think he would be the most honored of men. He was responsible for the beautiful buildings that were being built. His statue of Athena set the standard for all others. Surely, everyone would sing his praises.

"But, perhaps Phidias got carried away," continued my grandfather. "The Parthenon was elaborate and costly. His statue was huge and expensive. Maybe the people of Athens wondered if it was worth the great expense. City-states that paid large sums to Athens for protection questioned the cost of this grand display of wealth and power.

"Angry accusations were made. Phidias was charged with stealing gold that was meant for the statue of Athena. People also were shocked to discover that Phidias had put a portrait of himself and one of Pericles on Athena's shield. It was an act of disrespect to show a human face in such close connection to a god."

"So, did he steal the gold?" I asked again. "Did he commit a terrible act by putting himself and Pericles on the shield?"

"It's hard to say what really happened so long ago. The ancient writers said that Phidias had enemies who were jealous of him because he was so famous.

"Pericles had political enemies, too. Some of them thought that Pericles acted more like a king than a leader in a democratic state. They tried every way possible to bring him down. They attacked people close to him.

"They charged his wife, who had much more independence and power than other Greek women, with impiety, or wickedness. They charged an old teacher of Pericles with the same thing because, they said, he did not believe in gods. It was plain that accusing Phidias would also reflect poorly on Pericles.

"Phidias was eventually cleared of the charge of theft. He had wisely made the gold covering so it could be removed and weighed. When it was weighed, all the gold was there. As for the portraits, no one today really knows if the figures on Athena's shield represented Phidias and Pericles.

"But even so, some ancient writers said that Phidias was sent to prison, where he died. Others said he was sent far away. Recent discoveries made by archaeologists have disproved those stories. Phidias went on to another place after the Parthenon was finished. There he made yet another enormous masterpiece. His seated Zeus in the Temple of Olympia, near where the Olympic games were held, was considered one of the **seven wonders** of the ancient world."

People and Terms to Know

seven wonders—pyramids of Egypt, Hanging Gardens of Babylon, Phidias's statue of Zeus, temple of Artemis at Ephesus, tomb of Mausolus at Halicarnassus, Colossus of Rhodes, and the Pharos, or lighthouse, at Alexandria.

My grandfather reached into his pocket and handed me a small, worn, bronze-colored disk.

"This is a copy of an old Roman coin," he explained. "None of Phidias's original works exist today. Still, we can see a bit of his greatness in small pieces like this and in marble statues that were made by artists who saw and admired his work."

I looked closely at the hazy image and recognized Athena as she was carved at the Parthenon, spear in one hand and the Victory statue in the other.

"We can only imagine how she appeared to people who saw her in the dim light of the Parthenon," my grandfather said. "We can only guess what Phidias was trying to show with his monumental work. As you can see, we need imagination as well as knowledge to learn about people who lived long ago."

QUESTIONS TO CONSIDER

1. Why did Pericles decide to build great monuments in Athens?

2. Why was Phidias chosen to oversee the construction of the Parthenon?

3. What does this story tell you about how people in Athens felt about their city?

Euphronius and His Rival

BY STEPHEN CURRIE

There were no people like the Greeks. Thalassos and Timonium agreed on that. The Cretans, the Minoans, the Egyptians—they had their points, but they weren't *Greeks*.

And there were no artists like Greek artists, either. Thalassos and Timonium agreed on that, too. Greek poets, Greek musicians, Greek sculptors—all were so much better than artists from any other countries that it wasn't even funny.

And there were no Greek artists quite like potters. Thalassos and Timonium both thought so. "After all," Thalassos liked to say, "what can you *do* with a painting? Look at it; that's all. The same with a sculpture."

The krater was a pot for mixing wine with water. The Greeks usually drank their wine mixed like this.

"That's right," Timonium would agree, "but a pot is different. Not only is it pretty to look at, but it's useful."

Everybody, they agreed, had to eat and drink and cook and store things. Greek pottery was necessary, not just beautiful, especially when it was painted. The painting brought out the natural beauty of the pot itself. That was why they both collected pottery made by their fellow Greeks: goblets and cups, plates, jugs, and vases.

> *Greek pottery was necessary, not just beautiful, especially when it was painted.*

Unfortunately, that was all the agreement that Thalassos and Timonium were likely to have. Because the next question was always, "Who is the finest Greek potter?" And here they had very different ideas.

Timonium was sure the answer was **Euphronius**, known for pots with such a sense of flow that they almost seemed to take on life of their own. He was

---

People and Terms to Know

Euphronius (yoo•FROH•nee•uhs)—Greek potter and vase painter known to have worked during the 500s B.C. Today he is considered one of the greatest of all Greek artists.

▲

The shallow kylix was used as a drinking cup.

also the inventor of several new techniques that made pottery more interesting and longer lasting.

Thalassos was sure it was **Euthymides,** one of the first to use the modern **red-figure technique** of vase painting.

"It's Euthymides, you fool," Thalassos would snap. Timonium would reply that anyone *intelligent* knew it was really Euphronius, and Thalassos would shoot back that Euthymides had more creativity in his big toe than Euphronius had in his entire body. Timonium would call Thalassos an idiot.

People and Terms to Know

Euthymides (yoo•THIHM•uh•deez)—Greek potter and painter who lived and worked at roughly the same time as Euphronius.

red-figure technique—method of decorating pots. The designs were left in the red clay surface, and the backgrounds were painted black. The opposite method, in which the designs were painted in black on the red surface, is called black-figure technique.

And then, Thalassos would remind Timonium of Euthymides's **amphora.**

It really was quite a story, the tale of Euthymides's amphora. The potters of Athens, you understand, lived clustered in one neighborhood. Everywhere you looked, you saw people pumping foot pedals to turn the potter's wheels, putting paint on finished vases, and pawing through piles of wet clay. The sight and smell of clay were impossible to escape. There was wet mushy clay, soft gooey clay, hard brittle clay, clay in the ovens, clay on the hands of the potters.

> *Everywhere you looked, you saw people pumping foot pedals to turn the potter's wheels.*

Most of the potters were poor. Still, a few rose to fame. These men signed their work and sold it for many more **drachmas** than the average craftsman could command.

People and Terms to Know

amphora (AM•fuhr•uh)—two-handled jar for oil or wine.
drachmas (DRAK•muhs)—Greek money. In ancient Greece, a drachma was a silver coin.

No artists were better known than the two favored by Timonium and Thalassos. Most Greeks would have said Euphronius was the best, but there were many who would have chosen Euthymides. In some ways, they were almost equal. If you looked closely, though, you could find some differences. For example, Euphronius was more of a potter, while Euthymides was more of a painter. Likewise, Euthymides was more interested in painting scenes from daily life, while Euphronius preferred to show heroes. Everybody knew his paintings of Hercules in a wrestling match, of a horseman in full gallop, of people battling with monsters.

But we were talking about Euthymides's amphora. Euthymides, you see, was just a bit jealous of Euphronius. One time, Euthymides made a beautiful amphora and spent hours painting it. The result was truly beautiful. He was so proud that when he was finished, he added an extra line after his signature, which said:

"Euphronius never did anything *this* good."

It was a joke, some said, but to men like Thalassos and Timonium, it seemed a good deal more than that. Whenever the two collectors started calling each other fools and idiots, that was when Thalassos brought up the amphora.

"You see?" he'd crow. "Euthymides knew he was the best. And did Euphronius deny it? No, he did not!"

Whereupon Timonium would storm out, furious, promising never to talk to Thalassos again. But within a day or two, they would always calm down and get together again.

One afternoon Timonium showed up on Thalassos's doorstep, just hours after their latest argument. He was carrying a package and grinning from one ear all the way to the other, perhaps beyond.

◀ This kind of pot, called a *lekythos*, held precious oils and was often used by the Greeks as a funeral offering.

Thalassos was surprised to see his friend so soon after they'd quarreled, but he invited Timonium in. "Thank you," said Timonium politely, "but I'll just stand here for now. Tell me, Thalassos, who is the best artist in all the world?"

"That's easy," said Thalassos with a smirk. "It's Euthymides. *Obviously.*"

"Tell me, Thalassos, who is the best artist in all the world?"

Timonium only nodded. "Tell me again about the amphora," he suggested.

Thalassos was quite happy to repeat the story for what was probably the eighty-sixth time that year. So he did, quoting the writing on the bottom of the piece. He ended, as always, with "And did Euphronius deny it? No, he did not!"

"I see," said Timonium, and he reached to unfasten the parcel. "Then what, dear friend, do you say to *this*?"

He pulled out a cooking pot that was so achingly beautiful that it would have made most people's mouths water just to look at it. The pot seemed to shimmer and to dance, to shine and to sing. It had red-figure designs so gorgeous that they made Euthymides's pots look like the work of a child.

"Fresh from the potter's wheel and the oven and the paintbrush!" boasted Timonium. "I bought it this morning. Cost me a pretty drachma, it did, but be honest now—what do you say to *this*?"

Thalassos blinked his eyes, willing the pot to disappear. For weeks, months, years, he had always won the argument with Timonium. To himself, he had to admit that this pot was something special, but there was no way he would say it aloud. "Let me see it," he demanded.

"Enjoy." Timonium handed it over, whistling cheerfully.

Thalassos ran his fingers expertly over the pot's surface. The edges were smooth and sure, the thickness of the clay was as even as any potter could get. The designs were flawless. His heart sank. This was indeed a marvelous pot.

"Turn it over," Timonium invited.

Setting his jaw, Thalassos did exactly that. On the underside was an inscription: "Euphronius made me and painted me, too." And below that . . .

"What did your friend Euthymides put on that pot?" Timonium asked. "'Euphronius never did anything this good,' is that it?" He smiled again. "Well, here's the response."

With trembling fingers Thalassos found the words. "'Oh, yes, he did,'" he read aloud.

* * *

I would like to report that both the amphora and the cooking pot survive today, but I can't. I would also like to report that Thalassos and Timonium remained friends after that afternoon, but I can't do that either.

The truth is that while Euthymides's amphora can be found today in a museum in Germany, Euphronius's cooking pot is gone.

Ruined.

Smashed into a thousand tiny bits that day by Thalassos at his doorstep in Athens.

Which might explain why our two collectors never—and I do mean *never*—spoke to one another again.

QUESTIONS TO CONSIDER

1. Why was pottery important to the ancient Greeks?

2. Why do you think the question of which potter was better mattered so much to Thalassos and Timonium?

3. In what ways can Greek pottery tell us about the way people lived during those times?

Everyday Life:
The World of Ancient Greece
by Robert Hull

Robert Hull introduces many of the basic features of ancient Greek civilization, including political life, marriage and families, food, clothing, leisure time activities, health, and work.

A Greek Potter
by Giovanni Caselli

Giovanni Caselli describes the life and work of a typical potter and his family who live in Athens around 420 B.C.

Food and Feasts in Ancient Greece
by Imogen Dawson

Imogen Dawson introduces readers to life in ancient Greece by examining the food the people ate, where it came from, manners and customs, and the feasts and festivals that were celebrated.

Sources

The Palace at Knossos *by Walter Hazen*

Leander and the narrator of the story are fictitious characters. King Minos, Theseus, the Minotaur, Zeus, and Europa are all figures from Greek mythology. An excellent source for both the palace and Greek mythology is *The World of the Past,* edited by Jacquetta Hawkes (New York: Alfred A. Knopf, 1963).

A Story of Buried Treasure *by Barbara Littman*

Heinrich Schliemann's excavation of the city of Troy is a matter of historical fact. Information about it can be found in *In Search of the Trojan War* by Michael Wood (Berkeley: University of California Press, 1998) and in *The Greeks and Troy* by Deborah Tyler (New York: Dillon Press, 1993).

The Trojan War *by Judy Volem*

The human characters as well as the ancient gods who figure in this story are all from legends. Artifacts found at the site of Troy matched many of the details in the legend. The artifacts suggest that Troy was a wealthy and powerful city. It was built on land that could control the ship travel between the Black Sea and the Aegean Sea. Scholars today believe that a great war between Mycene and Troy took place there about 1250 B.C. and that some truth underlies the legend. It is told in two long poems, *The Iliad* and *The Odyssey.* Tradition says that *The Iliad* was written by the blind poet Homer. Modern scholars are not so sure. Probably Homer told, or sang, the stories and others wrote them down. Roman poet Virgil added the story of the Trojan horse in his long poem *The Aeneid.* There are many books in libraries that tell the story, and there are many scholarly works that discuss these epic poems. One book illustrated with drawings from ancient Greek vases and other artifacts is *Ancient Greek Literature in Its Living Context* by H. C. Baldry (New York, McGraw-Hill Book Company, 1968).

Contests with the Amazons *by Lynnette Brent*

Much of the information in "Contest with the Amazons" is based on legends preserved in the writings of the Greek historian Herodotus. However, archaeologists have found artifacts that point to the existence of Amazons. Records of these women give conflicting information. The ancient Greeks believed the Amazons lived near the mouth of the river Thermodon in northern Turkey. The ancient Roman historian Diodorus Siculus wrote about a race of Amazons living in the western part of Libya, in Africa. The information in this story is reflected in the book *On the Trail of the Women Warriors: The Amazons in Myth and History* by Lyn Webster Wilde (New York: St. Martin's Press, 2000).

Penelope and the Suitors *by Stephen Feinstein*

The story of Penelope is included in Homer's *Odyssey*. Sources for our story include *Daily Life in the Time of Homer* by Emile Mireaux (New York: Macmillan Company, 1959) and *The Odyssey of Homer* by Barbara Leonie Picard (New York: Henry Z. Walck, Inc., 1952).

The First Olympic Athletes *by Judith Lloyd Yero*

All people named in the story are historical people. Stories and quotations from ancient Greek texts are from *The Perseus Project* at Tufts University. This is a huge digital library of resources for the study of the ancient world. It includes texts from many original sources. It is available on CD or online at http://www.perseus.tufts.edu.

Treating the Sick *by Stephen Currie*

Cassia and Doctor Monacles are fictional characters. Hippocrates is a real person. The information about his methods and his ideas is historically accurate. You can find out more about Hippocrates in *Great Lives: Medicine* by Robert H. Curtis (New York: Scribners; Toronto: Maxwell MacMillan Canada; New York: Maxwell MacMillan International, 1993).

The Trial of Socrates *by Dee Masters*

The characters in the story are all historical figures. Socrates's teachings are preserved in the writings of his student Plato, among others. *The Horizon Book of Ancient Greece* by the Editors of *Horizon* magazine, William Harlan Hale author and editor in charge (New York: American Heritage Publishing company, Inc., 1965) includes the story of Socrates's trial and death.

Interview with a Spartan *by Walter Hazen*

Zethos the Spartan, and Alexandros the interviewer are fictional characters. So are Cassandra and Priamos, sister and brother to Zethos. King Leonidas and Lycurgus are real historical figures. Two sources for this story are *The Life of Greece,* by Will Durant (New York: Simon & Schuster, 1939) and *Everyday Life in Ancient Times* by Rhys Carpenter, Edith Hamilton, and others (Washington, DC, National Geographic Society, 1961).

Explorer from the Future by *Barbara Littman*

The space traveler and her Jump Masters are fictional. We know about Pericles and what Athens was like in his day from two primary sources. One is by the ancient Greek historian Thucydides (c. 460–400 B.C.) who commanded an expedition during the war and later wrote his *History of the Peloponnesian War.* The other comes from Plutarch. He was a Greek biographer who lived about 500 years later, from around A.D. 46–120. Plutarch wrote about Pericles in his work *Parallel Lives.* A modern source of information is *The Decline and Fall of Ancient Greece,* edited by Don Nardo (San Diego, CA: Greenhaven Press, 2000). Thucydides's work is available in *The Complete Writings of Thucydides: The Peloponnesian War,* the unabridged Crawley translation with an introduction by John H. Finley, Jr., Eliot Professor of Greek Literature, Harvard University (New York: The Modern Library).

Alexander the Great Tames His Horse *by Lynnette Brent*

The story's narrator is a fictional character. Alexander the Great and his father are real historical figures. The setting of the story is authentic, and the events are reported to have really happened. A good source for information about Alexander and his life is *Alexander of Macedon 356–323 B.C.: A Historical Biography* by Peter Green (Berkeley: University of California Press, 1991).

Aesop's Wonderful Fables *by Sharon Franklin*

The storyteller is a fictional character created by author Sharon Franklin. The fables are retellings of some of the stories traditionally associated with Aesop. There are many books about Aesop and many versions of his fables. A good book that includes not only Aesop's fables but also the works of such authors as Dickens, Shakespeare, and Baldwin is *The Book of Virtues for Young People: A Treasury of Great Moral Stories,* edited with commentary by William Bennett (Parsippany, NJ: Silver Burdett Press, 1996).

The Mystery of Phidias *by Judy Volem*

The narrator and the grandfather are fictional characters. Pericles and Phidias really lived, and Phidias's works have lasted to this day. More information about the Acropolis, the Parthenon, and Phidias's sculptures can be found in *The Parthenon* by Peter Green and the editors of the Newsweek Book Division (New York: Newsweek).

Euphronius and His Rival *by Stephen Currie*

Thalassos and Timonium are fictional characters. The information about Greek pottery is factually accurate, and Euphronius and Euthymides really lived. Many books of ancient Greek art include photographs of these beautiful pots. One especially nice one is *A Handbook of Greek Art: A Survey of the Visual Arts of Ancient Greece* by Gisela Richter (New York: Phaidon Paperback, 1969).

Glossary of People and Terms to Know

Achilles (uh•KIHL•eez)—hero of Homer's *Iliad* and the killer of Hector, the greatest Trojan warrior.

Acropolis (uh•KRAHP•uh•lihs)—high fortified place in Athens on which the Parthenon was built.

Aegean (ih•JEE•uhn) **Sea**—arm of the Mediterranean Sea between Greece and Turkey.

Aesop (EE•sahp)—Greek slave storyteller who lived about 500 B.C. Fables are intended to teach a lesson or show some truth.

Agamemnon (AG•uh•MEHM•nahn) —in Greek mythology, king of the Greek city of Mycenae (my•SEE•nee). He led the Greeks in the Trojan War.

agora (AG•uhr•uh)—ancient Greek marketplace.

Alexander—(356–323 B.C.) known as Alexander III and "Alexander the Great." He was king of Macedonia from 336 to 323 B.C. and conquered Asia Minor and the Middle East.

Amazon—in Greek legend, a member of a nation of women warriors.

amphora (AM•fuhr•uh)—two-handled jar for oil or wine.

Aphrodite (AF•ruh•DY•tee)—in Greek mythology, the goddess of love and beauty.

archaeology (AHR•kee•AHL•uh•jee) —finding and study of the remains of past human life. These remains might be graves, buildings, tools, jewelry, or pottery. The person who finds and studies these remains is called an *archaeologist* (AHR•kee•AHL•uh•jihst).

architects (AHR•kih•tehkts)—designers of buildings and other large structures.

Aristophanes (AR•ih•STAHF•uh•neez)—(c.448–c.388 B.C.) Athenian comic playwright.

Aristotle (AR•ih•STAHT•uhl)—(384–322 B.C.) Greek philosopher. Born in Macedonia, he went to Athens to study with Plato. He returned to Macedonia to tutor Alexander.

Athena (uh•THEE•nuh)—in Greek mythology, the goddess of wisdom.

Athens (ATH•uhnz)—city in the ancient region of Attica on the mainland of Greece, now the capital and largest city of Greece. People who live in Athens are called *Athenians* (uh•THEE•nee•uhnz).

Bucephalus (byoo•SEHF•uh•luhs) —Alexander the Great's war horse. The name means "bull-headed."

caduceus (kuh•DOO•see•uhs)—staff with two serpents twining around it. It is the symbol of the modern medical profession.

Cassandra (kuh•SAN•druh)—in Greek mythology, a daugher of King Priam of Troy. She could foretell the future, but no one ever believed her predictions.

cavalry (KAV•uhl•ree)—troops trained to fight on horseback.

city-states—independent states each consisting of a city and its surrounding territory. A city-state included the free men and women who were born there, foreigners, and slaves.

Crete (kreet)—island of southeast Greece in the eastern Mediterranean Sea. Its Minoan (my•NOH•uhn) civilization was one of the earliest in the world, reaching the height of its wealth and power c. 1600 B.C.

discus (DIHS•kuhs)—flat, circular plate or disk thrown for distance in athletic contests.

drachmas (DRAK•muhs)—Greek money. In ancient Greece, a drachma was a silver coin.

ethics (EHTH•iks)—rules or standards of right and wrong for a person or the members of a profession.

Euphronius (yoo•FROH•nee•uhs) —Greek potter and vase painter known to have worked during the 500s B.C. Today he is considered one of the greatest of all Greek artists.

Europa (yoo•ROH•puh)— legendary Phoenician princess. She was kidnapped by the god Zeus (who had changed himself into a white bull) and taken to Crete. Minos was their son. The continent of Europe is named for her.

Euthymides (yoo•THIHM•uh•deez) —Greek potter and painter who lived and worked at roughly the same time as Euphronius.

fresco (FREHS•koh)—painting on fresh moist plaster with colors dissolved in water.

Hector—son of Priam, king of Troy; the greatest of the Trojan warriors.

Helen—In Homer's *Iliad,* she is the wife of the king of Sparta. The Trojan War is said to have started because of her.

helots (HEHL•uhts)—people in Sparta who were neither slave nor free but farmed the estates of citizens. They could own property of their own, however. Since they outnumbered the citizens, they had to be kept from rebelling.

Hera (HEER•uh)—wife of Zeus, the chief Greek god.

Hercules (HUR•kyuh•LEEZ)—in Greek and Roman mythology, a son of Zeus. He was known for his strength and won immortality, or endless life, by performing 12 tasks demanded by Hera.

Herodotus (hih•RAHD•uh•tuhs)— (c.484–c.425 B.C.) Greek historian known as "the Father of History." He wrote a history of the war between the Greeks and the Persians.

Hippocrates (hih•PAHK•ruh•TEEZ) —(c.460–c.377 B.C.) Greek doctor called "the Father of Medicine."

Hippolyta (hih•PAHL•ih•tuh)— in Greek mythology, a queen of the Amazons. She was killed by Hercules.

Hisarlik (hih•sahr•LIHK)— modern site of ancient Troy in the present-day country of Turkey.

Homer (HOH•muhr)—Greek poet and author of two long poems, *The Iliad* and *The Odyssey,* written around 750 B.C. *The Iliad* tells of Troy and the Trojan War. *The Odyssey* tells of the adventures of Odysseus, king of Ithaca.

Iliad, The (see **Homer**)

Ithaca (IHTH•uh•kuh)—one of the Ionian Islands off western Greece and the legendary home of Odysseus and Penelope.

Knossos (NAHS•uhs)—ancient city of northern Crete and site of the remains of the famous palace of Knossos.

Kos (kahs)—island in the Aegean Sea off the southwest coast of Turkey.

Labyrinth (LAB•uh•rihnth)—in Greek mythology, the maze or group of complicated passageways where the hero Theseus killed the minotaur (MIHN•uh•tawr), a monster that had the head of a bull and the body of a man.

legend (LEHJ•uhnd)—story about great deeds handed down from the past. A legend cannot be proved to be true, but it is often believed by many people.

Leonidas (lee•AHN•ih•duhs)— (died 480 B.C.) Spartan king who led a small force against a huge Persian army at Thermopylae. All the Spartans were killed.

Lycurgus (ly•KUR•guhs)—Spartan lawmaker who lived in the 800s B.C.

Menelaus (MEHN•uh•LAY•uhs)—in Greek mythology, the king of Sparta at the time of the Trojan War and husband of Helen.

military dictatorship—type of government in which the armed forces have complete control.

Minos (MY•nuhs)—legendary king of Crete. He was said to be the son of Zeus, the supreme god of the Greeks, and Europa, a Phoenician princess. The ancient Greeks believed he had ruled several generations before the Trojan War, that is, around 1325 B.C.

Mount Olympus (see **Olympus**)

myth (mihth)—a story dealing with supernatural beings or heroes.

mythology (mih•THAHL•uh•jee) —group or collection of myths.

nomadic (noh•MAD•ihk)— related to people who move according to the seasons in search of food, water, and land for their animals to graze on.

Odysseus (oh•DIHS•yoos)—in Greek mythology, the king of Ithaca. The story of his adventures after the Trojan War is told in Homer's *Odyssey*.

Odyssey, The (see **Homer**)

Olympus (uh•LIHM•puhs)— highest point in Greece and the home of the mythical Greek gods.

Oracle (AWR•uh•kuhl) **of Delphi** (DEHL•fy)—shrine of the god Apollo in central Greece and the most sacred place in the Greek world. People went to Delphi to consult the priestess of Apollo, who revealed the god's answers to various questions. The answers were often puzzling.

Paris (PAIR•ihs)—son of the king of Troy. When he ran off with Helen, the Trojan War started.

Parthenon (PAHR•thuh•NAHN)— temple of the goddess Athena, guardian of Athens. It was begun in 447 B.C. and completed in 432. It is on the Acropolis

Patroclus (puh•TROH•kluhs)—in Greek mythology, a friend of Achilles. He was killed by Hector in the Trojan War.

Peloponnesian (PEHL•uh•puh•NEE•zhun) **War**— war between Athens and Sparta from 431 to 404 B.C.

Penelope (puh•NEHL•uh•pee)— faithful wife of Odysseus.

pentathlon (pehn•TATH•luhn)—athletic contest in which each participant competes in five track and field events.

Pericles (PEHR•ih•KLEEZ)—(c. 500–429 B.C.) Athenian statesman and general known for his speeches, his building program, and his democratic reforms. The period 460–429 B.C. is sometimes called the Periclean Age or the Golden Age of Athens.

Phidias (FIHD•ee•uhs)—(c.500–c.432 B.C.) Athenian sculptor considered the greatest artist of ancient Greece.

Philip—(382–336 B.C.) Philip II, king of Macedonia in northern Greece from 359 to 336. He was the father of Alexander the Great.

philosopher (fih•LAWS•uh•fuhr)—seeker of truth. The Greek word *philosophos* means "lover of knowledge."

plague (playg)—very dangerous disease that spreads rapidly and often causes death.

Priam (PRY•uhm)—in Greek mythology, the king of Troy, who was killed when his city fell to the Greeks.

red-figure technique—method of decorating pots. The designs were left in the red clay surface, and the backgrounds were painted black. The opposite method, in which the designs were painted in black on the red surface, is called black-figure technique.

sanctuary (SANGK•choo•EHR•ee)—sacred or holy place. At Olympia, the place of the Olympic games, it was a huge area made up of temples, altars, and other buildings.

Schliemann (SHLEE•mahn), **Heinrich** (HYN•rihk)—(1822–1890) German amateur archaeologist who discovered the ruins of ancient Troy.

Scythians (SIHTH•ee•uhns)—people who lived in an area that extended from the mouth of the Danube River on the Black Sea and on eastward.

seven wonders—pyramids of Egypt, Hanging Gardens of Babylon, Phidias's statue of Zeus, temple of Artemis at Ephesus, tomb of Mausolus at Halicarnassus, Colossus of Rhodes, and the Pharos, or lighthouse, at Alexandria.

siege (seej)—surrounding of a city by an army trying to capture it.

Socrates (SAHK•ruh•TEEZ)—(c.470–399 B.C.) famous Greek philosopher who used a question-and-answer method of teaching.

Sparta—city-state of ancient Greece. It was famous for its soldiers. The Spartans defeated Athens in the Peloponnesian (PEHL•uh•puh•NEE•zhuhn) War (460–404 B.C.).

stadium (STAY•dee•uhm)—large open area where the Olympic games were held. The nearly 200 meter length of the stadium at Olympia was the distance of the first Olympic race.

suitors—men who wanted to marry Penelope after her husband had been gone for ten years.

talent—unit of money used in ancient Greece, Rome, and the Middle East. A Greek talent was equal to about 58 pounds of a precious metal, such as silver or gold.

Telemachus (tuh•LEHM•uh•kuhs) —son of Penelope and Odysseus.

Thermopylae (thuhr•MAHP•uh•lee) —narrow pass through mountains in east-central Greece. It was the place of an unsuccessful Spartan stand against the Persians in 480 B.C.

Thucydides (thoo•SIHD•ih•DEEZ) —(c.460–c.400 B.C.) Greek historian considered the greatest historian of ancient times.

Troy—ancient city of northwest Asia Minor and the legendary place of the Trojan War. The people of Troy were called *Trojans*. The Trojan War between the Greeks and the Trojans lasted ten years. The ruins of Troy were first discovered by Heinrich Schliemann.

truce (troos)—temporary halt in a war.

Zeus (zoos)—in Greek mythology, god of the sky and king of the gods and human beings.

Acknowledgements

10 Bernard Cox/Bridgeman Art Library.
13 Erich Lessing/Art Resource, NY.
14 Corbis.
18 © Boltin Picture Library.
21 © Bettman/CORBIS.
24 © SuperStock.
27 Erich Lessing/Art Resource, NY.
31 © Scala/Art Resource, NY.
35 Hulton-Getty Picture Library.
39 © Scala/Art Resource, NY.
41 Hulton-Getty Picture Library.
43 © Bettman/CORBIS.
49 © Corbis.
51 © The Granger Collection.
52 © Corbis.
54 © Bettman/CORBIS.
57 © Stock Montage.
59 © Bettman/CORBIS.
63 © Aberdeen Art Gallery.
67 © Maicar Förlag-GML.
68 Réunion des Musées Nationaux/Art Resource/NY.
73 © Aberdeen Art Gallery.
75, 83 © Boltin Picture Library.
85 © Erich Lessing/Art Resource, NY.

93 From D'Aulaire's Book of Greek Myths by Ingri & Edgar Parin D'Aulaire. Copyright © 1962 by Ingri & Edgar Parin D'Aulaire. Used by permission of Random House Children's Books, a division of Random House, Inc.
94 © Erich Lessing/Art Resource, NY.
96 © Stock Montage.
107 © Burstein Collection/CORBIS.
114 Louvre, Paris, France/Bridgeman Art Library.
116 Tony Stone Images.
120 Museo Pio-Clementino Vaticano/Art Resource, NY.
127, 136 National Museum, Naples, Italy/A.K.G., Berlin/ SuperStock.
139 © North Wind Pictures.
142 © Stock Montage.
146 © North Wind Pictures.
148 © Bettman/CORBIS.
156 The Lowe Art Museum, The University of Miami/SuperStock.
158 © SuperStock.
165 The Lowe Art Museum, The University of Miami/SuperStock.